Pedro Lemebel

Chile's Defiant LGBTQ Writer – Unfiltered

Shanice Jiang

ISBN: 9781779697127
Imprint: Telephasic Workshop
Copyright © 2024 Shanice Jiang.
All Rights Reserved.

Contents

Introduction to Pedro Lemebel   1
Early life and upbringing   1
Activism and writing career   6
Personal life and relationships   13

Exposing LGBTQ Reality in Chile   19
Political and social context in Chile   19
The power of art as resistance   25
Confronting machismo and homophobia   30

Literary Contributions and Controversies   37
Early writing influences and inspirations   37
Critique of the Establishment   43
Controversies and censorship   49

Legacy and Impact   55
Influence on LGBTQ activism in Chile   55

Bibliography   59
Recognition and awards   61
Remembering Pedro Lemebel   65

Index   73

Introduction to Pedro Lemebel

Early life and upbringing

Childhood in Santiago, Chile

Pedro Lemebel was born on November 21, 1952, in the vibrant yet tumultuous landscape of Santiago, Chile. Growing up in a working-class family, Lemebel's early life was steeped in the socio-political realities of a nation grappling with inequality and oppression. Santiago, a city marked by stark contrasts, served as both a backdrop and a catalyst for his burgeoning identity and artistry.

In the heart of Santiago, Lemebel's childhood unfolded amidst the complexities of a post-colonial society. His family, rooted in the lower echelons of the socio-economic ladder, struggled to make ends meet. This environment instilled in him a profound awareness of social injustices from a young age. The streets of Santiago, bustling with life yet shadowed by poverty, became a crucible for his formative experiences. Lemebel often recalled how the cacophony of the city—the sounds of street vendors, the cries of children playing, and the distant echoes of political protests—shaped his perception of the world.

Lemebel's upbringing was further complicated by the conservative Catholic values that permeated Chilean society. These values often clashed with his emerging queer identity, leading to internal conflicts that would later manifest in his art and activism. The rigid expectations surrounding masculinity and sexuality in Santiago created a challenging environment for a young boy who felt different. He navigated a landscape where expressions of queerness were not only frowned upon but often met with hostility.

A pivotal moment in Lemebel's childhood occurred when he began to explore his identity through the arts. He was particularly drawn to the vibrant world of performance and literature, which offered him an escape from the confines of societal expectations. The influence of Chile's rich literary tradition—embodied by writers such as Pablo Neruda and Gabriela Mistral—ignited a spark within him. Lemebel's early encounters with literature provided a lens through which he could articulate his feelings of alienation and desire.

As he ventured into adolescence, the political climate in Chile began to shift dramatically. The rise of Salvador Allende's socialist government in the early 1970s brought with it a wave of hope and change, yet it also set the stage for profound societal upheaval. The promise of a more equitable society resonated with Lemebel, who was beginning to understand the intersections of his identity as a queer individual and a citizen of a politically charged nation. However, this hope was short-lived, as the military coup of 1973 led by Augusto Pinochet plunged Chile into a dark era of repression and violence.

The coup not only disrupted the political landscape but also had a profound impact on Lemebel's personal life. The ensuing dictatorship fostered an atmosphere of fear, silencing dissent and marginalizing those who dared to defy the status quo. As a teenager, Lemebel witnessed the brutal realities of state violence against those who challenged the regime, further solidifying his resolve to fight against oppression. The stark contrast between the vibrant cultural expressions of his youth and the somber realities of dictatorship would later inform his artistic voice.

In this turbulent environment, Lemebel's childhood was characterized by a duality—a longing for acceptance and a fierce defiance against societal norms. His experiences in Santiago, marked by both struggle and creativity, laid the groundwork for his future as a pioneering LGBTQ activist and writer. The streets that once echoed with the sounds of his childhood would later become the stage for his unapologetic performances, challenging the very fabric of Chilean society.

In summary, Pedro Lemebel's childhood in Santiago was a tapestry woven with threads of socio-economic struggle, political upheaval, and the quest for identity. These formative years not only shaped his worldview but also ignited a passion for activism that would define his life's work. As he navigated the complexities of growing up queer in a conservative society, Lemebel emerged as a voice for the marginalized, forever changed by the city that raised him.

Influence of his working-class background

Pedro Lemebel's journey as a writer and activist was profoundly shaped by his working-class background. Born in Santiago, Chile, in 1952, he grew up in a society marked by stark economic disparities and social hierarchies. The influence of his upbringing is not just a backdrop; it is a critical lens through which we can understand his artistic expression and political activism.

Socioeconomic Context

The landscape of Santiago during Lemebel's childhood was characterized by the struggles of the working class. The economic conditions of the time forced many families, including Lemebel's, to navigate a world rife with poverty and limited opportunities. The Chilean society of the 1950s and 1960s was dominated by a capitalist framework that often marginalized those from lower socioeconomic backgrounds. This context of hardship instilled in Lemebel a sense of defiance and a desire to challenge the status quo.

Art as a Reflection of Class Struggle

Lemebel's writing and performances often reflect the struggles of the working class. He utilized his art as a means of resistance against the oppressive structures that sought to silence marginalized voices. For instance, his early works are infused with the rawness of street life, capturing the essence of the struggles faced by the LGBTQ community within the broader context of class oppression. This intersectionality is crucial; Lemebel's narratives often highlight how class and sexuality intersect, revealing the complexities of identity in a society that seeks to impose rigid norms.

$$C = \frac{S}{T} \tag{1}$$

Where C represents class consciousness, S signifies social struggle, and T denotes the transformative potential of art. Lemebel's works exemplify how art can elevate class consciousness, fostering a collective identity among those marginalized by both class and sexuality.

Personal Experiences and Identity Formation

Growing up in a working-class neighborhood, Lemebel was acutely aware of the societal expectations placed on him as a queer individual. His experiences of bullying and discrimination were not only rooted in his sexual identity but also intertwined with his socioeconomic status. This duality of oppression informed his worldview and shaped his voice as a writer.

Lemebel's defiance against societal norms can be seen in his decision to embrace his queer identity openly. This act of self-acceptance was revolutionary in a culture that often stigmatized both poverty and homosexuality. By refusing to conform, Lemebel challenged the dominant narratives that sought to marginalize him, using his background as a source of strength rather than shame.

Collective Identity and Activism

Lemebel's working-class background also fostered a sense of solidarity with others who faced similar struggles. His involvement in the LGBTQ rights movement in Chile was not merely a personal endeavor; it was a collective fight for dignity and recognition. The founding of the performance collective "Yeguas del Apocalipsis" exemplifies this spirit of collaboration. Through this collective, Lemebel and his peers used performance art to confront societal norms and advocate for LGBTQ rights, creating a platform that amplified their voices.

The group's performances often drew from their shared experiences as working-class individuals, using humor and satire to critique the societal structures that oppressed them. This approach not only challenged the conservative values prevalent in Chile but also fostered a sense of community among those who felt alienated by mainstream society.

Conclusion

In conclusion, Pedro Lemebel's working-class background was a significant influence on his identity, writing, and activism. His experiences shaped his understanding of the intersectionality of class and sexuality, allowing him to articulate the struggles of the LGBTQ community in a way that resonated deeply with others. By embracing his identity and using his art as a tool for resistance, Lemebel not only challenged the oppressive structures of his time but also paved the way for future generations of activists and artists to continue the fight for equality and acceptance.

Through his life and work, Lemebel remains a testament to the power of art as a vehicle for social change, illustrating how the struggles of the working class can inspire a defiant and unapologetic quest for justice.

Discovery of his queer identity

Pedro Lemebel's journey toward embracing his queer identity was as vibrant and tumultuous as the streets of Santiago, where he grew up. Born in the heart of a society steeped in conservative Catholic values, Lemebel's early life was a battleground of internal and external conflicts, where the struggle for self-acceptance clashed with societal expectations.

From a young age, Lemebel felt different. He was acutely aware of the rigid gender roles imposed upon him and the expectations that accompanied them. In Chilean culture, these norms were not just suggestions; they were mandates that dictated behavior, aspirations, and even dreams. The concept of masculinity was often intertwined with machismo, a cultural trait that glorified aggression,

EARLY LIFE AND UPBRINGING

dominance, and heterosexuality. For Lemebel, who was sensitive and expressive, this environment felt suffocating.

As he navigated his childhood in Santiago, Lemebel began to explore his identity through the lens of art and performance. This exploration was not merely a personal journey; it was also a radical act of defiance against the oppressive structures surrounding him. In his writings and performances, he began to articulate the complexities of his queer identity, challenging the binary notions of gender and sexuality that dominated Chilean society.

The influence of his working-class background played a crucial role in shaping his understanding of identity. Growing up in a socioeconomically disadvantaged environment, Lemebel witnessed firsthand the intersections of class, sexuality, and societal marginalization. This perspective allowed him to recognize the systemic inequalities that affected not only his life but also the lives of countless others in the LGBTQ community. His experiences fueled his desire to confront these injustices, leading him to embrace his identity with pride.

Lemebel's discovery of his queer identity was not without its challenges. Coming out to his family and friends was a pivotal moment in his life, marked by both fear and hope. He faced the possibility of rejection from those he loved, a fear that is all too common in the LGBTQ community. Yet, in the face of this fear, he found strength in authenticity. By living openly as a queer man, he not only liberated himself but also inspired others to embrace their true selves.

The societal backlash against LGBTQ individuals in Chile during the 1970s and 1980s was severe. Homophobia was rampant, and many faced violence and discrimination for their sexual orientation. Lemebel's experiences during this time were reflective of the broader struggles faced by the LGBTQ community. The oppressive political climate under Pinochet's regime further complicated matters, as dissent against the government often intersected with dissent against sexual minorities. The fear of persecution loomed large, but Lemebel's resolve only grew stronger.

Art became Lemebel's weapon of choice in this fight for identity and acceptance. Through his provocative performances and writings, he challenged the status quo, using his platform to bring visibility to the often-invisible struggles of LGBTQ individuals. His work served as a mirror reflecting the harsh realities of society while simultaneously offering a glimpse of the beauty found in queer existence.

One notable example of this is his performance art, where he often donned flamboyant costumes and engaged in acts that defied traditional gender norms. These performances were not merely for shock value; they were deeply symbolic acts of rebellion against a culture that sought to silence and erase queer identities.

By embracing the theatricality of his persona, Lemebel carved out a space for himself and others like him, asserting that their lives and identities were worthy of celebration.

In his writings, Lemebel employed a raw and unapologetic style, often laced with humor and satire. He tackled themes of love, desire, and the complexity of queer relationships, laying bare the joys and pains of being a gay man in a repressive society. His literary contributions became a vital part of the LGBTQ narrative in Chile, providing solace and inspiration to those grappling with their own identities.

The discovery of his queer identity was not a singular moment but rather an ongoing process of self-realization and acceptance. It was a journey marked by pain, joy, and an unwavering commitment to authenticity. Lemebel's courage to embrace his identity in the face of adversity laid the groundwork for his future activism, as he became a beacon of hope for many in the LGBTQ community.

Ultimately, Pedro Lemebel's discovery of his queer identity was a testament to the power of self-acceptance and the importance of living one's truth. His journey serves as a reminder that the fight for identity and acceptance is not just a personal battle but a collective struggle that requires courage, resilience, and a fierce commitment to challenging societal norms. In embracing his identity, Lemebel not only transformed his own life but also ignited a movement that would inspire generations to come.

Activism and writing career

Joining the LGBTQ rights movement in Chile

Pedro Lemebel's journey into the LGBTQ rights movement in Chile was not just a personal awakening but a powerful response to the oppressive socio-political landscape of his time. Emerging from the shadows of a conservative society steeped in Catholic values, Lemebel became a beacon of hope and defiance for the LGBTQ community. His entrance into activism was marked by a profound understanding of the intersectionality of identity, culture, and politics.

The Political Landscape

In the 1980s, Chile was under the authoritarian regime of Augusto Pinochet, a period characterized by severe human rights violations and a repressive atmosphere for any form of dissent. The LGBTQ community faced systemic discrimination, often subjected to violence and persecution. The prevailing machismo culture further marginalized queer identities, reinforcing a societal norm that deemed homosexuality as taboo. Lemebel, acutely aware of these dynamics, recognized that the fight for LGBTQ rights was intrinsically linked to broader struggles for human rights and social justice.

Activism Begins

Lemebel's activism began to take shape in the late 1980s when he joined the burgeoning LGBTQ rights movement in Chile. He was not just a passive observer; he actively sought to challenge the status quo. His involvement was rooted in a desire to articulate the lived experiences of queer individuals, particularly those from working-class backgrounds like himself. This perspective was vital in a movement often dominated by more privileged voices, allowing him to bring a unique lens to the struggles faced by marginalized communities.

Founding "Yeguas del Apocalipsis"

In 1991, Lemebel co-founded the performance art collective "Yeguas del Apocalipsis" (Mares of the Apocalypse), a group that would become instrumental in the fight for LGBTQ visibility and rights in Chile. The collective was known for its provocative performances that blended art with activism, challenging societal norms and confronting the pervasive homophobia entrenched in Chilean culture. Through their art, they sought to reclaim public spaces, making bold statements about identity, sexuality, and resistance.

The performances of the Yeguas were often controversial, pushing boundaries and provoking dialogue. For instance, their iconic act of dressing in flamboyant attire and parading through the streets of Santiago was a direct challenge to the conservative values that sought to silence them. These acts were not merely for shock value; they were strategic, aimed at drawing attention to the injustices faced by the LGBTQ community. Lemebel's ability to intertwine humor, satire, and raw emotion in these performances made them resonate deeply with audiences, both within and outside the LGBTQ community.

Impact on LGBTQ Rights

Lemebel's contributions to the LGBTQ rights movement in Chile extended beyond performance art. His written works served as a powerful tool for advocacy, articulating the struggles and aspirations of queer individuals. Through his essays and literary pieces, he exposed the harsh realities of life for LGBTQ individuals in a repressive society. His work challenged readers to confront their biases and question the societal norms that perpetuated discrimination.

One notable example of his impact was the publication of his book, *Loco Afán: Crónicas de Sidario*, which compiled a series of essays reflecting on the AIDS crisis and its devastating effects on the LGBTQ community in Chile. This work not only highlighted the urgent need for awareness and action but also humanized the experiences of those affected by the epidemic. Lemebel's candid and unapologetic writing style resonated with many, inspiring a new generation of activists to take up the mantle of advocacy.

Challenges Faced

Despite his significant contributions, Lemebel faced numerous challenges as an activist. The oppressive political climate of Chile meant that LGBTQ activism was often met with hostility. Activists were frequently targeted by law enforcement, and public demonstrations were often met with violence. Lemebel himself experienced harassment and threats, yet he remained undeterred. His resilience in the face of adversity became emblematic of the broader struggle for LGBTQ rights in Chile.

Moreover, the internal challenges within the LGBTQ community were equally daunting. Lemebel was vocal about the need for inclusivity and acceptance within the movement, often critiquing the elitism that permeated certain activist circles. He believed that true progress could only be achieved through solidarity and unity among all members of the LGBTQ community, regardless of class, race, or gender identity.

Conclusion

Pedro Lemebel's entry into the LGBTQ rights movement in Chile marked the beginning of a transformative journey that would leave an indelible mark on the landscape of activism. His unique blend of art, literature, and activism not only challenged societal norms but also inspired countless individuals to embrace their identities and fight for their rights. As he navigated the complexities of activism in a repressive environment, Lemebel emerged as a formidable force, advocating for a world where love and acceptance could flourish in the face of adversity. His legacy continues to inspire new generations of activists, reminding us that the fight for LGBTQ rights is far from over.

Founding the collective "Yeguas del Apocalipsis"

In the vibrant tapestry of Chile's LGBTQ activism, few threads are as bold and irreverent as those woven by Pedro Lemebel and his collective, "Yeguas del

Apocalipsis." Founded in the early 1990s, this avant-garde group emerged as a radical response to the oppressive socio-political climate of post-dictatorship Chile, where the remnants of Pinochet's regime still cast long shadows over the rights and identities of marginalized communities. The collective's name, which translates to "Mares of the Apocalypse," evokes a sense of both urgency and defiance, encapsulating their mission to challenge societal norms and confront the injustices faced by the LGBTQ community.

The Birth of Yeguas del Apocalipsis

Lemebel, alongside fellow artists and activists, created Yeguas del Apocalipsis as a platform for performance art that would disrupt the status quo and provoke critical conversations about gender, sexuality, and identity. Drawing inspiration from a variety of sources, including punk rock, drag culture, and the vibrant street art scene, the collective sought to create a space where queer voices could be amplified and celebrated. Their performances often took place in public spaces, transforming everyday locations into stages for their unapologetic expressions of identity and resistance.

One of the defining characteristics of Yeguas del Apocalipsis was their use of camp aesthetics and humor to subvert traditional notions of masculinity and femininity. By embracing flamboyance and exaggeration, the collective not only challenged societal expectations but also created a sense of solidarity among LGBTQ individuals who felt alienated by mainstream culture. Their performances were a celebration of queer identity, a rejection of heteronormativity, and a call to arms for those who had been marginalized.

Art as a Form of Resistance

The collective's performances were not merely artistic expressions; they were acts of political defiance. In a society where conservative Catholic values still held sway, Yeguas del Apocalipsis used art to confront and dismantle the deeply entrenched machismo and homophobia that permeated Chilean culture. Through their provocative performances, they addressed issues such as sexual violence, discrimination, and the struggle for LGBTQ rights, often drawing attention to the stark realities faced by queer individuals in a society that sought to silence them.

For example, one of their most notable performances, "La Muerte de un Hombre Bueno" (The Death of a Good Man), critiqued the societal expectations placed on men and the violence that often resulted from toxic masculinity. By staging a mock funeral for the archetype of the "good man," the collective highlighted the absurdity of these expectations and the harm they inflicted on both men and women. This performance, like many others, sparked controversy and debate, challenging audiences to confront their own complicity in perpetuating harmful norms.

Challenges and Controversies

Despite their artistic success, Yeguas del Apocalipsis faced significant challenges and backlash from conservative factions within Chilean society. Their explicit and provocative content often drew the ire of traditionalists, leading to clashes with authorities and attempts to censor their performances. These confrontations underscored the precarious position of LGBTQ activists in a society still grappling with its past and reluctant to embrace change.

Moreover, the collective's commitment to addressing issues of social justice extended beyond the LGBTQ community. They recognized the intersections of race, class, and gender in their activism, advocating for a more inclusive and equitable society. This intersectional approach was groundbreaking in a context where many LGBTQ movements focused primarily on issues of sexual orientation and gender identity.

Impact on LGBTQ Activism and Culture

The legacy of Yeguas del Apocalipsis is profound. They not only paved the way for future generations of LGBTQ activists and artists in Chile but also contributed to a broader cultural shift towards acceptance and inclusivity. Their fearless approach to performance art inspired countless individuals to embrace their identities and challenge societal norms, fostering a sense of community and solidarity among those who had been marginalized.

As Lemebel once stated, "To be a queer artist in Chile is to be a warrior." This sentiment encapsulates the spirit of Yeguas del Apocalipsis and their unwavering commitment to fighting for justice and equality. Through their art, they created a space for dialogue, resistance, and empowerment, leaving an indelible mark on the landscape of LGBTQ activism in Chile and beyond.

In conclusion, the founding of Yeguas del Apocalipsis was a pivotal moment in the history of Chilean LGBTQ activism. By harnessing the power of performance art as a tool for resistance, Pedro Lemebel and his collective challenged societal norms, confronted discrimination, and inspired a movement that continues to resonate today. Their legacy serves as a reminder of the transformative potential of

Impact of his written works on activism

Pedro Lemebel's literary contributions transcended mere storytelling; they became powerful tools for activism that ignited a movement within the LGBTQ community in Chile and beyond. His works resonated deeply with the struggles faced by marginalized individuals, challenging societal norms and inspiring a collective consciousness that demanded change. This section explores the profound impact of Lemebel's writings on activism, focusing on three key areas: the mobilization of the LGBTQ community, the challenge to societal norms, and the international resonance of his messages.

Mobilization of the LGBTQ Community

Lemebel's writings served as a rallying cry for LGBTQ individuals in Chile. His unapologetic exploration of queer identity and experiences provided a voice to those who had long been silenced. Through works such as *Libnando en la Oscuridad* and *Los Heterosexuales*, he articulated the pain and resilience of living as a queer person in a repressive society. His prose was infused with raw emotion, capturing the essence of the struggle against discrimination and violence.

One of the most significant impacts of Lemebel's work was its ability to mobilize individuals towards activism. His narratives often included calls to action, urging readers to confront their realities and challenge the status quo. For instance, in his performance art, he frequently addressed the audience directly, transforming passive observers into active participants in the fight for LGBTQ rights. This direct engagement not only fostered a sense of community but also galvanized individuals to take part in protests, advocacy, and collective action.

Challenging Societal Norms

Lemebel's writings were not just a reflection of LGBTQ experiences but also a fierce critique of societal norms that perpetuated discrimination. His sharp wit and incisive satire targeted the machismo culture prevalent in Chilean society, exposing the toxic masculinity that often led to violence against queer individuals. In his essay *"La Ciudad de los Hombres"*, he dismantled the facade of traditional masculinity, arguing that it was a construct designed to oppress not only women but also men who deviated from heteronormative standards.

By challenging these deeply ingrained societal norms, Lemebel opened up dialogues about gender and sexuality that were previously considered taboo. His work encouraged readers to question their beliefs and the societal structures that upheld discrimination. This critical examination of culture was instrumental in fostering a more inclusive environment, as it empowered individuals to confront their biases and advocate for change.

International Resonance of His Messages

While Lemebel's primary focus was on the Chilean context, the themes present in his work resonated with LGBTQ communities worldwide. His exploration of identity, love, and resistance transcended geographical boundaries, creating a universal narrative of the struggle for acceptance and rights. For example, his poignant reflections on love and loss in the face of oppression found echoes in the experiences of LGBTQ individuals in various cultural contexts.

Moreover, Lemebel's work has been instrumental in shaping global conversations around LGBTQ rights. His provocative style and fearless critiques of power structures inspired activists beyond Chile, encouraging them to adopt similar strategies in their own movements. The impact of his writings can be seen in the way contemporary LGBTQ literature often embraces boldness and confrontation, echoing Lemebel's legacy of defiance.

Conclusion

In conclusion, Pedro Lemebel's written works significantly impacted LGBTQ activism by mobilizing the community, challenging societal norms, and resonating on an international scale. His ability to articulate the struggles of queer individuals with passion and clarity not only inspired a generation of activists but also transformed the landscape of LGBTQ rights in Chile. As we continue to navigate the complexities of identity and activism, Lemebel's contributions remind us of the power of words to incite change and foster resilience in the face of adversity. His legacy endures, encouraging future generations to embrace their identities and fight for equality with the same fervor and defiance that he exemplified throughout his life.

Personal life and relationships

Exploring his sexuality and relationships

Pedro Lemebel's journey through his sexuality and relationships is a vivid tapestry woven with threads of defiance, desire, and discovery. Growing up in Santiago, Chile, during a time when societal norms were rigidly defined by conservative values, Lemebel's exploration of his queer identity was not merely a personal endeavor; it was an act of rebellion against the oppressive structures surrounding him.

From a young age, Lemebel exhibited a profound awareness of his differences. His childhood in a working-class neighborhood exposed him to both the harsh realities of life and the vibrant spectrum of human experience. This duality became a crucible for his identity, shaping his understanding of love and attraction. As he navigated the complexities of his emerging sexuality, Lemebel faced the daunting challenge of reconciling his desires with the expectations of a society steeped in machismo and heteronormativity.

The process of coming out to himself was tumultuous. Lemebel's early relationships were marked by secrecy and fear, often conducted in the shadows of societal disapproval. He found solace in clandestine encounters, where the thrill of forbidden love mingled with the stark reality of potential ostracization. This dichotomy is poignantly captured in his writings, where he often juxtaposes the ecstasy of love against the backdrop of societal rejection.

$$\text{Self-Acceptance} = \text{Desire} + \text{Fear} - \text{Societal Norms} \qquad (2)$$

In his later years, Lemebel's relationships evolved into a more public assertion of his identity. He embraced the idea that love, in all its forms, was worthy of celebration. His romantic partnerships were not merely personal; they became political statements that challenged the status quo. He often spoke about the importance of visibility in the LGBTQ community, asserting that love should not be confined to the shadows but rather paraded with pride.

Lemebel's exploration of his sexuality also intersected with his activism. He recognized that his personal experiences were emblematic of a larger struggle faced by many in the LGBTQ community. His relationships were often infused with a sense of urgency, as he sought to create spaces where love could flourish without fear. The relationships he cultivated were not just about intimacy; they were about solidarity and resistance against a society that sought to marginalize queer identities.

One notable relationship that shaped Lemebel's understanding of love was with fellow artist and activist, Francisco Casas. Their partnership was characterized by a shared commitment to challenging societal norms and advocating for LGBTQ rights. Together, they formed a formidable alliance, using their art as a vehicle for activism. Their bond illustrated the power of love as a catalyst for change, reinforcing the idea that personal relationships could transcend individual desires and contribute to a collective struggle for justice.

However, Lemebel's path was not without its challenges. The societal stigma surrounding homosexuality in Chile often manifested in violence and discrimination, impacting his relationships profoundly. The fear of persecution loomed large, forcing many queer individuals, including Lemebel, to navigate their love lives with caution. He experienced heartbreak and loss, yet these experiences fueled his resolve to fight for a world where love could exist freely, unencumbered by societal constraints.

In his writings, Lemebel eloquently articulated the complexities of love within the LGBTQ context. He penned poignant narratives that explored the intersections of desire, identity, and societal expectation. His work served as both a mirror and a window, reflecting the struggles of many while offering a glimpse into the possibility of liberation through love.

Through his exploration of sexuality and relationships, Lemebel not only forged his identity but also illuminated the path for others. He became a beacon of hope for those grappling with their own desires in a world that often rejected them. His legacy is a testament to the power of love as a transformative force—one that challenges oppression and celebrates the beauty of human connection in all its forms.

In conclusion, Pedro Lemebel's exploration of his sexuality and relationships was a profound journey marked by both personal and political dimensions. His experiences reflect the broader struggles faced by the LGBTQ community in Chile, revealing the intricate interplay between love, identity, and activism. As we delve into his life, we uncover not only the story of a remarkable individual but also the enduring fight for love and acceptance in a world that continues to grapple with its complexities.

Coming out to his family and friends

Coming out is a multifaceted journey that often involves navigating the complexities of personal identity, familial relationships, and societal expectations. For Pedro Lemebel, this journey was no different. Growing up in Santiago, Chile, where conservative values often dominated social discourse, the act of coming out was not merely a personal revelation but a defiant statement against the prevailing norms of machismo and heteronormativity.

The Context of Coming Out

In the context of Chile during the late 20th century, coming out was fraught with risks. The societal backdrop was marked by a history of political oppression, particularly during the Pinochet regime, which not only stifled dissent but also marginalized LGBTQ voices. The stigma attached to homosexuality was pervasive, often leading to familial rejection, social ostracism, and violence. According to [?], the fear of familial backlash is a common barrier for many LGBTQ individuals in conservative societies.

Pedro's upbringing in a working-class family added another layer of complexity. The expectations placed upon him were shaped by economic struggles and traditional values, which often prioritized conformity over individuality. As he began to understand and embrace his queer identity, he faced the daunting task of reconciling this identity with his family's expectations.

The Coming Out Process

Pedro's coming out was not a singular event but rather a gradual process. He initially confided in close friends who were part of the burgeoning LGBTQ community in Santiago. This support system became crucial as he navigated his identity, offering him a safe space to express himself without the fear of judgment. According to [?], the role of friends in the coming out process can significantly mitigate feelings of isolation and fear.

When it came to his family, however, the stakes were higher. Pedro's decision to come out to his family was marked by trepidation. He understood that revealing his identity could lead to rejection, yet he also recognized that living authentically was essential for his mental well-being. The moment he chose to disclose his sexuality to his mother is particularly poignant. He recounted this experience in his writings, illustrating the tension between love and fear.

> "I told her, 'Mamá, I like men.' The silence that followed was deafening. It was as if the air had been sucked out of the room. But then she looked at me, and in her eyes, I saw a flicker of understanding."

This moment encapsulated the dual nature of coming out: the liberation of self-acceptance weighed against the potential for familial estrangement.

Challenges Faced

The challenges Pedro faced were not solely external. Internally, he grappled with feelings of shame and fear, which are common in many coming out narratives. The psychological impact of living in a society that devalues one's identity can lead to what [?] describes as "minority stress," a chronic stress faced by marginalized individuals.

Pedro also confronted the reality of rejection. Not all family members were accepting, and the fear of losing loved ones loomed large. He experienced moments of painful disconnection, particularly with relatives who adhered strictly to conservative values. This rejection, however, did not deter him from his path; instead, it fueled his activism and writing, pushing him to advocate for acceptance and understanding within the broader Chilean society.

The Impact of Coming Out

Ultimately, coming out was a transformative experience for Pedro. It not only solidified his identity as a queer man but also positioned him as a vocal advocate for LGBTQ rights in Chile. His willingness to share his story helped to illuminate the struggles faced by many in the LGBTQ community, fostering a sense of solidarity among those who felt similarly marginalized.

Pedro's coming out narrative exemplifies the broader struggles of LGBTQ individuals in conservative societies. It highlights the importance of authenticity, the need for supportive networks, and the ongoing fight for acceptance and equality. As he once poignantly stated, "To be visible is to resist."

In conclusion, Pedro Lemebel's journey of coming out to his family and friends was emblematic of the larger LGBTQ experience in Chile. It served as a catalyst for his activism and a source of inspiration for countless others navigating their own paths toward self-acceptance. The courage to be unapologetically oneself is a powerful act of resistance, one that Pedro embodied throughout his life.

Challenges and triumphs in his love life

Pedro Lemebel's journey through love was as vibrant and tumultuous as his activism. Growing up in Santiago, amidst the oppressive shadows of a conservative society, he faced unique challenges that shaped his romantic experiences. The intersection of his queer identity and his socio-political environment created a landscape where love was both a source of joy and a battleground for acceptance.

Navigating Societal Norms

In a country where traditional values dominated, Lemebel's exploration of his sexuality was fraught with danger. The prevailing machismo culture not only marginalized queer identities but also perpetuated violence against them. Lemebel's relationships were often complicated by societal expectations, leading to a constant negotiation between his authentic self and the roles imposed by society.

To illustrate this struggle, consider the theory of *heteronormativity*, which posits that heterosexuality is the default or norm, thereby marginalizing non-heterosexual relationships. This framework can be applied to Lemebel's experiences, where his love life was often a rebellion against the norms that sought to confine him. He openly challenged these constraints, seeking partners who understood and embraced his defiance.

Love as Resistance

Despite these challenges, Lemebel found love that transcended societal boundaries. He often engaged in relationships with other artists and activists, creating a community that fostered mutual support and understanding. His love life became a form of resistance, a way to assert his identity and claim space within a hostile environment.

One notable relationship was with a fellow artist, whose shared passion for performance art ignited a profound connection. Together, they explored the depths of their identities, intertwining their lives and art. This partnership not only provided emotional support but also fueled Lemebel's creative output, leading to some of his most provocative works.

Coming Out and Family Dynamics

Coming out to family and friends was another significant challenge in Lemebel's love life. His relationship with his family was complex; while some members were supportive, others struggled to accept his identity. This duality created a tension that often influenced his romantic relationships.

For example, when he came out to his mother, he faced a mixture of love and disappointment. This moment was pivotal, as it highlighted the societal pressures that many LGBTQ individuals face when seeking acceptance. Lemebel's ability to navigate these familial dynamics showcased his resilience and determination to live authentically, despite the potential for familial estrangement.

Triumphs in Love

Amidst the challenges, Lemebel experienced profound triumphs in his love life. His relationships often served as a source of inspiration, leading to a deeper understanding of himself and his art. The passion he found in love translated into his writings, where he celebrated the beauty and complexity of queer relationships.

In his work, Lemebel often depicted love as an act of rebellion. He wrote candidly about his encounters, infusing his narratives with raw emotion and unfiltered honesty. This approach not only resonated with readers but also contributed to a broader dialogue about queer love in a conservative society. His writings became a testament to the idea that love, in all its forms, is a powerful force for change.

Conclusion

In summary, Pedro Lemebel's love life was marked by challenges that reflected the broader societal issues faced by the LGBTQ community in Chile. Yet, through these struggles, he triumphed, finding love that inspired his art and activism. His relationships were not merely personal experiences; they were acts of defiance against a world that sought to silence him. By embracing his identity and celebrating his love, Lemebel carved a path for future generations of LGBTQ individuals to follow, proving that love, indeed, knows no boundaries.

Exposing LGBTQ Reality in Chile

Political and social context in Chile

Historical discrimination against the LGBTQ community

The LGBTQ community in Chile has faced a long and tumultuous history of discrimination, rooted in a combination of cultural, religious, and political factors. This section will explore the historical context that has shaped the experiences of LGBTQ individuals in Chile, highlighting key moments, societal attitudes, and the systemic challenges that have persisted over decades.

Colonial and Post-Colonial Context

The roots of discrimination against LGBTQ individuals in Chile can be traced back to colonial times, when the Spanish imposed their patriarchal and heteronormative values upon the indigenous populations. The arrival of the Spanish conquistadors in the 16th century brought with it a rigid set of moral codes influenced by the Catholic Church, which condemned non-heteronormative behaviors as sinful and deviant. The indigenous practices of same-sex relationships were largely suppressed, and those who deviated from the established norms faced severe penalties.

In the post-colonial era, the consolidation of the Chilean state in the 19th century further entrenched these discriminatory attitudes. The legal framework, heavily influenced by the Napoleonic Code, criminalized homosexual acts, reflecting a broader societal view that equated homosexuality with immorality and social decay. Articles of the Penal Code, such as *Article 365*, explicitly targeted homosexual acts, leading to arrests, public shaming, and ostracism of individuals identified as LGBTQ.

20th Century Developments

The 20th century saw a continuation of these discriminatory practices, particularly during the military dictatorship of Augusto Pinochet from 1973 to 1990. The regime implemented a campaign of terror against perceived enemies of the state, which included LGBTQ individuals. Homosexuality was criminalized, and many LGBTQ individuals were subjected to torture, imprisonment, and forced disappearances. The political climate fostered an environment of fear, where LGBTQ individuals were forced to conceal their identities to survive.

During this period, a significant event that marked the intersection of LGBTQ rights and political activism was the 1984 assassination of the gay activist *Joaquín Lavín*, a prominent figure in the fight for LGBTQ rights. His death served as a rallying point for the community, highlighting the urgent need for visibility and resistance against systemic oppression.

Post-Dictatorship Era and Legal Battles

Following the end of the dictatorship, the 1990s ushered in a new era of hope and activism for the LGBTQ community. However, the remnants of historical discrimination continued to shape societal attitudes. The transition to democracy did not immediately translate into legal protections for LGBTQ individuals. Activists faced the daunting task of challenging deeply ingrained prejudices and advocating for legal reforms.

In 1999, the first LGBTQ pride parade was held in Santiago, marking a significant milestone in the visibility of the community. However, the event was met with backlash from conservative groups, who viewed it as an affront to traditional values. This tension illustrated the ongoing struggle between progressive movements advocating for LGBTQ rights and conservative factions seeking to maintain the status quo.

Legal battles for recognition and rights continued into the 21st century. In 2004, the Chilean government proposed a civil union law that would grant some legal rights to same-sex couples. However, the law faced fierce opposition from conservative political and religious groups, delaying its passage for several years. The eventual approval of the law in 2015 was a significant step forward, yet it did not fully address the systemic discrimination faced by LGBTQ individuals.

Contemporary Issues and Ongoing Discrimination

Despite advancements in legal recognition, discrimination against the LGBTQ community remains pervasive in Chile. Reports of hate crimes, discrimination in employment, and social ostracism continue to plague LGBTQ individuals. The influence of conservative Catholic values persists, often manifesting in political rhetoric that marginalizes LGBTQ voices.

For instance, the 2017 legislative debates surrounding the legalization of same-sex marriage revealed deep societal divides. Conservative lawmakers argued that such measures would undermine the traditional family structure, while LGBTQ activists highlighted the need for equality and recognition of diverse family forms.

Furthermore, the intersectionality of discrimination must be acknowledged, as LGBTQ individuals from marginalized racial and socio-economic backgrounds often face compounded challenges. The systemic nature of discrimination can be represented mathematically as follows:

$$D_{LGBTQ} = f(S, R, E) \qquad (3)$$

Where:

- D_{LGBTQ} represents the level of discrimination faced by LGBTQ individuals.
- S is the societal attitudes towards LGBTQ individuals.
- R is the level of legal recognition and rights afforded to LGBTQ individuals.
- E is the economic status and opportunities available to LGBTQ individuals.

This equation illustrates that discrimination is a multifaceted issue, influenced by societal norms, legal frameworks, and economic conditions.

In conclusion, the historical discrimination against the LGBTQ community in Chile has been shaped by a complex interplay of cultural, political, and social factors. From colonial times to the contemporary era, LGBTQ individuals have faced significant challenges in their quest for recognition and equality. Understanding this historical context is crucial for appreciating the ongoing struggles and resilience of the LGBTQ community in Chile as they continue to fight for their rights and dignity in a society that has often marginalized them.

Influence of conservative Catholic values

The conservative Catholic values that permeate Chilean society have played a significant role in shaping attitudes toward the LGBTQ community. These values are deeply rooted in the country's history, culture, and social norms, often manifesting as opposition to LGBTQ rights and identities. The Catholic Church, as a dominant institution in Chile, has historically wielded considerable influence over public policy, education, and personal beliefs, thus impacting the lived experiences of LGBTQ individuals.

Historical Context

To understand the influence of conservative Catholic values, it is essential to consider Chile's historical context. Following the Spanish colonization, Catholicism became the state religion, embedding religious doctrine into the fabric of Chilean identity. The Church's teachings on sexuality, marriage, and family have reinforced heteronormative standards, marginalizing those who do not conform. This historical backdrop created a societal framework that often views LGBTQ identities as deviant or sinful.

Theological Underpinnings

The Catholic Church's stance on homosexuality is grounded in specific theological interpretations. Traditional Catholic doctrine holds that sexual relations are only permissible within the confines of heterosexual marriage, aimed at procreation. This belief is articulated in texts such as the *Catechism of the Catholic Church*, which states that homosexual acts are "intrinsically disordered" and contrary to natural law. Consequently, LGBTQ individuals are often subjected to moral condemnation, leading to internalized homophobia and societal ostracism.

Political Influence

The political influence of conservative Catholic values is evident in legislative processes and public policy. For instance, the Church has actively opposed initiatives aimed at advancing LGBTQ rights, including same-sex marriage and anti-discrimination laws. The 2015 legalization of civil unions for same-sex couples in Chile was a contentious issue, with the Church mobilizing against it, arguing that such measures undermine the sanctity of traditional marriage. This resistance highlights the Church's role as a powerful actor in shaping public discourse and policy decisions.

Social Implications

The social implications of conservative Catholic values extend beyond politics into everyday life. LGBTQ individuals often face discrimination, harassment, and violence, rooted in the belief that their identities are morally unacceptable. For example, a study conducted by the *Movilh* (Movimiento de Integración y Liberación Homosexual) revealed that 70% of LGBTQ respondents reported experiencing discrimination in various forms, including verbal abuse and physical violence. Such experiences are exacerbated by the Church's teachings, which perpetuate stigma and foster an environment of fear and isolation.

Resistance and Resilience

Despite the oppressive influence of conservative Catholic values, LGBTQ activists like Pedro Lemebel have emerged as powerful voices of resistance. Lemebel's works often critique these values, exposing the hypocrisy of a society that claims to uphold moral standards while perpetuating violence and discrimination against marginalized communities. Through performance art, literature, and public demonstrations, he challenged the status quo, creating space for dialogue and fostering a sense of community among LGBTQ individuals.

Conclusion

In conclusion, the influence of conservative Catholic values in Chile has significantly impacted the LGBTQ community, shaping societal attitudes, political landscapes, and individual experiences. The historical and theological underpinnings of these values have fostered an environment of discrimination and marginalization. However, the resilience of activists like Lemebel serves as a testament to the enduring struggle for acceptance and equality. As Chile continues to navigate the complexities of LGBTQ rights, the interplay between conservative values and progressive movements will remain a critical area of examination.

Legal battles for LGBTQ rights

The journey towards LGBTQ rights in Chile has been fraught with challenges, marked by a series of legal battles that reflect the broader socio-political landscape of the country. These struggles have not only been about the recognition of rights but also about the fight against deeply entrenched societal norms and prejudices.

Historical Context

The legal framework surrounding LGBTQ rights in Chile has evolved significantly over the past few decades. Under the dictatorship of Augusto Pinochet (1973-1990), homosexuality was criminalized, and LGBTQ individuals faced severe persecution. The regime's oppressive policies created an environment of fear, forcing many into silence. This historical backdrop is crucial for understanding the subsequent legal battles that activists like Pedro Lemebel would face.

Key Legal Developments

The post-dictatorship era saw the gradual emergence of LGBTQ rights in Chile, beginning with the decriminalization of homosexuality in 1999. However, this was just the first step in a long and arduous journey. Activists pushed for anti-discrimination laws, marriage equality, and the recognition of LGBTQ families.

One pivotal moment in the legal landscape was the introduction of the *Ley de Identidad de Género* (Gender Identity Law) in 2018, which allowed transgender individuals to change their legal gender without undergoing surgery. This law was a significant victory for the community, yet it highlighted ongoing challenges, such as the lack of comprehensive anti-discrimination protections.

Challenges in the Legal System

Despite these advancements, legal battles remain ongoing, often hindered by conservative opposition. The Chilean legal system has been slow to adapt to the needs of the LGBTQ community, with many cases of discrimination going unpunished. For instance, a 2021 report from the *Movilh* (Movimiento de Integración y Liberación Homosexual) highlighted numerous instances of hate crimes against LGBTQ individuals, with many victims reluctant to report incidents due to fear of retribution or disbelief.

Moreover, the fight for marriage equality faced significant hurdles. Although the law was finally passed in December 2019, the journey was marked by intense debates in Congress and widespread public opposition fueled by conservative religious groups. This exemplifies the broader societal resistance that LGBTQ activists have had to confront.

The Role of Activism in Legal Battles

Activism has played a crucial role in advancing legal rights for LGBTQ individuals in Chile. Organizations like *Yeguas del Apocalipsis*, co-founded by Lemebel, utilized performance art as a means of protest, drawing attention to the injustices faced by the community. Their work not only challenged societal norms but also pressured lawmakers to take action.

In addition to grassroots activism, legal advocacy has been essential. Lawyers and activists have collaborated to file lawsuits challenging discriminatory practices and advocating for policy changes. For example, the *Ley de Matrimonio Igualitario* (Marriage Equality Law) was the result of years of persistent lobbying and public demonstrations, showcasing the power of collective action.

Conclusion

The legal battles for LGBTQ rights in Chile illustrate a complex interplay of societal attitudes, historical context, and the tireless efforts of activists. While significant progress has been made, the fight is far from over. As Pedro Lemebel's legacy continues to inspire new generations, the ongoing struggle for equality and justice remains a testament to the resilience of the LGBTQ community in Chile. The legal landscape may have shifted, but the quest for true acceptance and rights is an unfinished journey, demanding vigilance and unwavering commitment.

The power of art as resistance

Lemebel's use of performance art to challenge societal norms

Pedro Lemebel, a luminary in the realm of LGBTQ activism, masterfully wielded performance art as a potent weapon against the oppressive societal norms that pervaded Chilean culture. His performances transcended mere artistic expression; they became acts of defiance, confronting the rigid expectations imposed by a society steeped in conservative values and machismo.

At the heart of Lemebel's approach was the idea that performance art could serve as a visceral critique of the status quo. Drawing on the theories of performance as a site of resistance, such as those proposed by theorists like Judith Butler and Peggy Phelan, Lemebel's work embodied the notion that identity is not a fixed essence but rather a series of performances that can be subverted and redefined. Butler's concept of gender performativity, which posits that gender is constructed through repeated actions and behaviors, resonates deeply with Lemebel's artistic philosophy. By embracing and exaggerating queer identities in his performances, Lemebel not only challenged societal norms but also invited his audience to reconsider their own perceptions of gender and sexuality.

Lemebel's performances often took place in public spaces, transforming mundane environments into arenas of radical expression. One notable example is his piece titled "La Piel de Chile" (The Skin of Chile), where he donned extravagant costumes and makeup, embodying the flamboyance and resilience of the LGBTQ community. This performance was not merely for shock value; it was a direct confrontation to the hyper-masculine ideals that dominated Chilean society. By subverting traditional gender roles, Lemebel created a space where vulnerability and strength coexisted, challenging the audience to reflect on their own biases and assumptions.

Furthermore, Lemebel's use of language in his performances was equally impactful. He often employed a blend of poetry and spoken word, weaving narratives that highlighted the struggles and triumphs of queer individuals in a heteronormative society. His ability to articulate the pain of exclusion and the joy of self-acceptance resonated with many, fostering a sense of solidarity within the LGBTQ community. For instance, in his performance "El Último Suspiro" (The Last Sigh), Lemebel recited poignant verses that spoke to the experiences of those marginalized by both society and the state. This blending of art and activism not only amplified the voices of the oppressed but also served to educate and provoke thought among those outside the community.

The impact of Lemebel's performances extended beyond the immediate audience. His work sparked conversations about the intersections of art, politics, and identity, challenging spectators to confront their complicity in maintaining oppressive structures. In a society where LGBTQ individuals were often silenced, Lemebel's art became a rallying cry for change, inspiring others to embrace their identities and advocate for their rights.

Moreover, Lemebel's performances often addressed the complexities of machismo and homophobia within Chilean culture itself. He was unafraid to critique not only the external societal pressures but also the internalized prejudices that existed within the LGBTQ community. This dual critique is crucial in understanding the depth of his work; it reveals a commitment to fostering an inclusive environment that acknowledges and addresses all forms of discrimination. For example, in his performance "Las Yeguas del Apocalipsis," he and his collaborators used satire to expose the contradictions of machismo, illustrating how toxic masculinity harms not only women and LGBTQ individuals but also men themselves. By employing humor and absurdity, Lemebel was able to engage audiences in difficult conversations about masculinity, vulnerability, and acceptance.

In conclusion, Pedro Lemebel's use of performance art was a revolutionary act that challenged societal norms and ignited conversations about identity, sexuality, and resistance. His ability to blend personal narrative with broader social critique created a powerful platform for LGBTQ advocacy, making his work not only relevant but essential in the ongoing fight for equality. Through his performances, Lemebel left an indelible mark on the cultural landscape of Chile, inspiring generations to embrace their true selves and confront the societal structures that seek to confine them. The legacy of his art continues to resonate, reminding us of the transformative power of performance as a tool for social change.

Performances that sparked controversy and conversation

Pedro Lemebel's performances were more than mere expressions of art; they were incendiary acts of defiance that challenged the status quo of Chilean society. In a country where the LGBTQ community faced systemic discrimination and societal scorn, Lemebel's art became a powerful tool for resistance, igniting conversations that many wished to avoid. His performances, often laced with provocative imagery and biting satire, pushed boundaries and exposed the underbelly of machismo and homophobia entrenched in Chilean culture.

One of Lemebel's most notable performances was *El Ladrón de Bicicletas* (The Bicycle Thief), where he donned a flamboyant costume and recited poetry that intertwined personal narratives with critiques of societal norms. This performance, held in public spaces, was not just a showcase of talent; it was a bold statement against the oppressive forces that marginalized queer identities. The choice of a public venue was deliberate, as it forced audiences to confront uncomfortable truths about their own biases and the realities of LGBTQ life in Chile.

The backlash from conservative sectors was immediate and fierce. Critics accused Lemebel of promoting indecency and undermining traditional values. However, this controversy only fueled the fire of conversation around LGBTQ rights, with Lemebel's supporters arguing that his performances were essential to breaking the silence surrounding queer issues. The tension between Lemebel and his detractors exemplified the cultural clash in Chile, where traditional Catholic values often clashed with the burgeoning LGBTQ rights movement.

Another significant performance was *La Historia de la Homosexualidad en Chile* (The History of Homosexuality in Chile), which Lemebel used to narrate the struggles and victories of the LGBTQ community through a blend of storytelling, music, and visual art. This performance was particularly controversial as it directly addressed the historical erasure of queer voices in Chilean history. By reclaiming this narrative, Lemebel not only honored those who came before him but also challenged audiences to acknowledge the ongoing struggles faced by LGBTQ individuals.

The impact of these performances extended beyond the immediate audience. They were often documented and discussed in the media, leading to broader public discourse on LGBTQ issues. Lemebel's work resonated with many, sparking a wave of artistic responses from other queer artists and activists who sought to continue the conversation he had ignited.

Moreover, Lemebel's performances often included elements of camp and irony, which served to disarm audiences and invite them into a dialogue rather than a confrontation. His use of humor allowed him to address serious topics without alienating those who might be resistant to more straightforward critiques. This strategy was rooted in the theory of *queer performativity*, which posits that performance can be a site of identity formation and resistance. By embodying queer identities in his performances, Lemebel not only asserted his own identity but also created a space for others to explore and express their queerness.

However, not all responses were positive. Many conservative figures labeled his performances as an affront to public morality, leading to attempts to censor his work. In one instance, a performance was abruptly canceled due to threats from local politicians, highlighting the precarious position of LGBTQ artists in a society that often views their existence as a challenge to its moral fabric. This censorship only served to amplify Lemebel's message, demonstrating the urgent need for visibility and representation in the arts.

In conclusion, Pedro Lemebel's performances were pivotal in sparking controversy and conversation around LGBTQ issues in Chile. Through his bold and unapologetic art, he challenged societal norms, confronted machismo, and provided a voice for the voiceless. His legacy is a testament to the power of performance as a medium for activism, illustrating how art can provoke thought, inspire change, and ultimately reshape cultural narratives. The conversations he initiated continue to resonate, reminding us that the fight for LGBTQ rights is far from over and that art remains a vital tool in this ongoing struggle.

Impact on the LGBTQ community and broader society

Pedro Lemebel's work transcended the boundaries of literature and performance art, acting as a powerful catalyst for change within the LGBTQ community in Chile and beyond. His audacious performances and writings challenged societal norms, igniting conversations that were often deemed taboo in a country steeped in conservative values. Lemebel's impact can be understood through several dimensions: the empowerment of the LGBTQ community, the transformation of public discourse, and the reshaping of cultural narratives.

Empowerment of the LGBTQ Community

Lemebel's unapologetic expression of his queer identity provided a voice to many who felt marginalized and voiceless. His performances, characterized by flamboyant aesthetics and provocative themes, resonated deeply with the LGBTQ community, fostering a sense of pride and solidarity. By boldly confronting societal expectations, Lemebel inspired individuals to embrace their identities and challenge the stigma associated with being queer.

One notable example of this empowerment was his participation in the collective "Yeguas del Apocalipsis," which he co-founded. The group utilized performance art as a form of protest, often staging interventions in public spaces that highlighted the struggles faced by LGBTQ individuals. Their work was not merely artistic; it was a declaration of existence and resistance. Through their performances, they created a safe space for self-expression and solidarity, encouraging others to join the fight for acceptance and equality.

Transformation of Public Discourse

Lemebel's art also played a crucial role in transforming public discourse surrounding LGBTQ issues in Chile. His writings, often laced with satire and social commentary, challenged the status quo and questioned the deeply ingrained machismo and homophobia prevalent in Chilean society. By addressing these issues head-on, Lemebel forced the public to confront uncomfortable truths about discrimination and inequality.

The impact of his work is evident in the way it opened up dialogues about sexuality, identity, and rights. His explicit and provocative style, while controversial, served to draw attention to the realities faced by the LGBTQ community. For instance, his literary piece "La esquina de los sueños" (The Corner of Dreams) painted a vivid picture of the struggles and aspirations of queer individuals, compelling readers to empathize with their experiences. This shift in discourse contributed to a gradual change in societal attitudes, paving the way for increased visibility and acceptance of LGBTQ people in Chile.

Reshaping Cultural Narratives

Beyond activism and discourse, Lemebel's influence extended to reshaping cultural narratives surrounding queerness. He challenged the heteronormative frameworks that dominated Chilean literature and art, introducing a queer perspective that had been largely absent. His unique style, which blended personal narrative with broader social critique, created a new literary space for LGBTQ voices.

The legacy of Lemebel's work can be seen in the emergence of a new generation of queer writers and artists in Chile, who draw inspiration from his unapologetic approach. His influence is evident in contemporary literature that explores themes of identity, love, and resistance, often echoing Lemebel's boldness in confronting societal norms. This cultural shift not only honors Lemebel's contributions but also ensures that the struggles and triumphs of the LGBTQ community remain at the forefront of Chilean cultural discourse.

Conclusion

In conclusion, Pedro Lemebel's impact on the LGBTQ community and broader society is profound and multifaceted. Through his fearless performances and writings, he empowered marginalized voices, transformed public discourse on LGBTQ issues, and reshaped cultural narratives in Chile. Lemebel's legacy continues to inspire activism and artistic expression, reminding us of the power of art as a tool for resistance and the importance of visibility in the ongoing fight for equality. His work stands as a testament to the resilience of the LGBTQ community and the enduring struggle for acceptance and rights in a world that often seeks to silence them.

Confronting machismo and homophobia

Lemebel's critique of toxic masculinity in Chilean culture

Pedro Lemebel's work is a powerful critique of toxic masculinity, particularly as it manifests within the context of Chilean culture. Toxic masculinity refers to cultural norms that promote a narrow definition of manhood, often characterized by aggression, emotional repression, and a disdain for anything perceived as feminine. In Chile, these norms have been deeply entrenched, often reinforced by a combination of historical, social, and political factors.

Lemebel's critique can be understood through the lens of several key theoretical frameworks. One relevant approach is R.W. Connell's concept of hegemonic masculinity, which describes the dominant form of masculinity that is culturally exalted and often associated with power, control, and heterosexuality. This framework is particularly useful in analyzing how Lemebel exposes the ways in which these ideals are not only harmful to women and LGBTQ individuals but also to men themselves, who are pressured to conform to these restrictive roles.

In his performances and writings, Lemebel often subverts traditional masculine ideals by embracing vulnerability and fluidity in gender expression. For instance, in his provocative piece "El deseo de la mujer" (The Desire of the Woman), he challenges the hypermasculine archetype by openly expressing desire and affection towards both men and women. This act of defiance against established norms creates a space for dialogue about the limitations imposed by toxic masculinity, allowing for a broader understanding of gender and sexuality.

Moreover, Lemebel's use of humor and satire serves as a tool to critique the absurdity of these toxic norms. In his performance art, he often adopts exaggerated masculine personas only to dismantle them through comedic exaggeration. This technique not only highlights the performative nature of masculinity but also invites audiences to reflect on their own complicity in upholding these harmful standards.

A significant example of this critique can be found in his work "La mujer en el espejo" (The Woman in the Mirror), where Lemebel juxtaposes the image of the macho man with that of the effeminate man, challenging the audience to reconsider their perceptions of masculinity. He articulates the pain and isolation that many men experience when they fail to meet societal expectations, illustrating how these pressures can lead to violence, both towards others and oneself.

Lemebel also confronts the intersections of toxic masculinity and homophobia within the LGBTQ community. He critiques how some men within the community perpetuate the very norms they seek to escape, often engaging in misogynistic behaviors or shaming those who do not conform to traditional masculine standards. This internalized homophobia is a significant barrier to achieving true inclusivity and acceptance within the community.

Furthermore, Lemebel's work is situated within the broader context of Chilean history, where the legacy of dictatorship and repression has contributed to a culture of machismo. The Pinochet regime's authoritarian rule not only enforced rigid gender roles but also perpetuated violence against those who challenged these norms. Lemebel's activism and writing serve as a counter-narrative to this oppressive history, advocating for a more inclusive understanding of gender and sexuality that rejects toxic masculinity.

In conclusion, Pedro Lemebel's critique of toxic masculinity in Chilean culture is multifaceted and deeply impactful. By employing humor, satire, and personal narrative, he exposes the limitations of traditional masculine ideals and the harm they inflict on individuals and society as a whole. His work encourages a reevaluation of masculinity, advocating for a more compassionate and inclusive understanding that embraces vulnerability and rejects violence. Through his fearless exploration of these themes, Lemebel not only challenges the status quo but also inspires future generations to continue the fight against toxic masculinity and for LGBTQ rights in Chile and beyond.

Confronting homophobia within the LGBTQ community itself

The LGBTQ community, often perceived as a unified front against discrimination and prejudice, is not immune to internal conflicts and biases. Among these, homophobia—defined as the aversion to or discrimination against individuals based on their sexual orientation—can manifest within the very community that advocates for acceptance and equality. Pedro Lemebel, through his life and work, boldly confronted these issues, shedding light on the complexities of identity and the intersections of oppression.

Understanding Internalized Homophobia

Internalized homophobia refers to the internalization of societal homophobic attitudes by LGBTQ individuals, leading to self-hatred and prejudice against others within the community. This phenomenon can be traced back to the pervasive stigma surrounding homosexuality, often exacerbated by cultural and societal norms. Lemebel's writings frequently explore this theme, illustrating how the pressures of conformity to heteronormative standards can lead to self-rejection among queer individuals.

For example, in his performance art, Lemebel would often adopt exaggerated feminine personas, challenging the rigid constructs of masculinity that are prevalent not only in society at large but also within the LGBTQ community itself. By doing so, he highlighted how even those who identify as queer can perpetuate harmful stereotypes against more marginalized identities, such as transgender individuals or those who do not conform to traditional gender roles.

Machismo and Its Impact

In Chile, machismo—a cultural concept that valorizes traditional masculine traits—plays a significant role in shaping attitudes within the LGBTQ community. Lemebel critiqued this toxic masculinity, arguing that it not only harms women but also constrains men who identify as gay. He posited that the pressure to conform to hyper-masculine ideals leads some gay men to adopt homophobic attitudes towards others, particularly towards effeminate men or those who do not fit the mold of traditional masculinity.

The internal conflict faced by individuals who navigate their sexual identity while grappling with societal expectations can lead to a hierarchy within the LGBTQ community. This hierarchy often privileges certain identities over others, creating divisions that undermine the collective struggle for equality. Lemebel's work serves as a reminder that the fight against homophobia must also include an examination of how we treat one another within our own community.

Examples of Internal Conflict

Lemebel's own experiences reflect the struggles many LGBTQ individuals face. In his memoirs and essays, he recounts instances where he encountered prejudice from other queer individuals, particularly regarding his flamboyant style and unapologetic expression of his identity. These encounters reveal a painful truth: that acceptance is not always guaranteed within the community itself.

One notable example is the backlash he received from more conservative members of the LGBTQ community who believed that his provocative art and outspoken nature harmed the broader movement for rights. This tension illustrates the ongoing struggle to define what it means to be part of the LGBTQ community and who gets to represent that identity.

The Role of Activism in Addressing Internal Homophobia

Lemebel's activism was not solely focused on external oppressors; he also sought to address the internalized prejudices within the LGBTQ community. He believed that confronting homophobia in all its forms was essential for genuine solidarity. By using his platform to challenge both societal norms and internal biases, Lemebel encouraged open dialogue about the complexities of identity.

Through his performances and writings, he fostered a sense of awareness about the importance of inclusivity and acceptance among all members of the LGBTQ community. He advocated for embracing diversity, emphasizing that the strength of the movement lies in its ability to uplift marginalized voices rather than silencing them.

Conclusion

In conclusion, confronting homophobia within the LGBTQ community is a multifaceted challenge that requires introspection and dialogue. Pedro Lemebel's legacy serves as a powerful reminder that the fight for equality must encompass not only external battles against societal discrimination but also internal struggles against prejudice and exclusion. By embracing the full spectrum of identities within the LGBTQ community, activists can forge a more inclusive and effective movement, one that honors the complexities of human experience and fosters solidarity among all individuals, regardless of their sexual orientation or gender identity.

Pushing boundaries for acceptance and inclusivity

Pedro Lemebel's work transcended mere artistic expression; it was a clarion call for acceptance and inclusivity within both the LGBTQ community and Chilean society at large. In a cultural landscape marred by machismo and homophobia, Lemebel's performances and writings served as radical interventions that challenged prevailing norms and pushed the boundaries of what was considered acceptable.

At the core of Lemebel's activism was the concept of **intersectionality**, which posits that various forms of social stratification, such as race, class, and gender, do not exist separately from one another but are interwoven together. This framework allowed Lemebel to critique not only the external societal pressures faced by the LGBTQ community but also the internalized homophobia and misogyny that could exist within it. For instance, in his performance art, Lemebel often donned feminine attire, thereby subverting traditional gender roles and challenging the rigid expectations of masculinity that permeated Chilean culture. His boldness in embracing femininity was both a personal declaration and a political statement, asserting that all expressions of identity deserve validation.

One of Lemebel's most powerful contributions to the discourse on inclusivity was his willingness to confront the **toxic masculinity** prevalent in Chilean society. He articulated how machismo not only oppressed women but also marginalized men who did not conform to heteronormative standards. In his essay "La esquina de los sueños" (The Corner of Dreams), he vividly illustrated the struggles faced by queer individuals who navigated a world that demanded conformity to rigid masculine ideals. By exposing the fragility of these ideals, Lemebel invited audiences to reconsider their definitions of strength and vulnerability.

Moreover, Lemebel's critique extended to the LGBTQ community itself, where he often highlighted the instances of discrimination and exclusion that occurred within its ranks. He argued that the struggle for acceptance must encompass all identities, including those that are often sidelined, such as transgender and non-binary individuals. In his work, he called for a more inclusive movement that recognized the diversity of experiences within the LGBTQ spectrum. This was particularly evident in his collective, **Yeguas del Apocalipsis**, which not only embraced queer identities but also sought to amplify the voices of those who faced multiple layers of oppression.

Lemebel's performances often sparked controversy, yet they were instrumental in fostering dialogue about acceptance and inclusivity. For example, his 1994 performance titled El Canto de la Resistencia (The Song of Resistance) featured a provocative blend of drag, poetry, and political commentary. In this piece, he donned a wedding dress and recited verses that celebrated love while simultaneously critiquing the societal norms that dictated who could love whom. The performance ignited discussions about the legitimacy of queer love and the right to express it openly, challenging audiences to confront their biases.

In addition to his artistic endeavors, Lemebel's writings, such as *Lihn's Letters*, served as a platform for pushing boundaries. Through his unapologetic prose, he addressed issues of desire, identity, and the societal constraints that hindered personal freedom. His work not only resonated with LGBTQ individuals but also reached allies and those outside the community, broadening the conversation about inclusivity.

Lemebel's legacy is evident in the ongoing fight for LGBTQ rights in Chile and beyond. His insistence on pushing boundaries has inspired a new generation of activists who continue to advocate for a more inclusive society. The emergence of movements that address intersectionality within LGBTQ activism can be traced back to the groundwork laid by Lemebel and his contemporaries.

In conclusion, Pedro Lemebel's relentless pursuit of acceptance and inclusivity was not merely an artistic endeavor; it was a life mission. By confronting societal norms, challenging internalized prejudices, and advocating for the recognition of diverse identities, Lemebel pushed the boundaries of what it meant to be part of the LGBTQ community in Chile. His work remains a vital part of the ongoing struggle for equality, reminding us that the fight for acceptance is far from over.

Literary Contributions and Controversies

Early writing influences and inspirations

Exploration of Chile's literary tradition

The literary tradition of Chile is rich and multifaceted, characterized by a blend of indigenous influences, colonial legacies, and modernist aspirations. It serves as a backdrop for understanding the emergence of voices like Pedro Lemebel, whose contributions to literature and activism reflect both the complexities and the vibrancy of this tradition.

Historical Context

Chile's literary landscape can be traced back to the colonial period, where the influence of Spanish literature intermingled with indigenous oral traditions. The early works of writers such as *Alonso de Ercilla* and *Pablo Neruda* showcase the tension between colonization and cultural identity. Ercilla's epic poem *La Araucana*, written in the 16th century, exemplifies the complexities of colonial encounters, depicting the resistance of the Mapuche people against Spanish conquest. This historical context is crucial for understanding the evolution of Chilean literature as it relates to themes of identity, resistance, and cultural hybridity.

19th Century Developments

The 19th century marked a significant transformation in Chile's literary tradition with the emergence of the *Generación del 38*, a group of writers who sought to establish a national literature that reflected Chilean realities. Notable figures such as *Joaquín Edwards Bello* and *Alfredo B. Palacio* contributed to the development of a literary canon that emphasized the importance of local themes and characters. Their works often critiqued societal norms and addressed issues of class and identity, paving the way for future generations of writers, including Lemebel.

Modernism and the Avant-Garde

The modernist movement in Chile, marked by the works of poets like *Neruda* and *Gabriela Mistral*, introduced new forms and styles that broke away from traditional conventions. This period saw a flourishing of poetic expression that embraced themes of love, politics, and existentialism. The avant-garde movements of the early 20th century further challenged established norms, with writers exploring surrealism and experimental forms. Lemebel's work can be seen as a continuation of this avant-garde spirit, utilizing innovative narrative techniques and performance art to confront societal issues.

Queer Literature and Identity

The exploration of queer identity within Chilean literature is a relatively recent development, emerging alongside the broader LGBTQ rights movement. Writers such as *María Luisa Bombal* and *Alberto Fuguet* began to address issues of sexuality and gender in their works, setting the stage for Lemebel's unapologetic exploration of queer themes. His writings not only reflect his personal experiences but also challenge the heteronormative narratives that have dominated Chilean literature. Lemebel's unique voice resonates with the struggles of marginalized communities, making his work a vital part of Chile's literary tradition.

Influence of Political Turmoil

The political landscape of Chile, particularly during the dictatorship of Augusto Pinochet, profoundly impacted its literary tradition. The repression of dissenting voices led to a flourishing of underground literature and the emergence of writers who used their craft as a form of resistance. Lemebel's work is deeply rooted in this context, as he navigated the complexities of living as an openly gay man during a time of extreme societal repression. His writings often serve as a critique of the political establishment, blending personal narrative with social commentary.

Contemporary Voices and Legacy

In recent years, the resurgence of LGBTQ literature in Chile has brought new voices to the forefront, continuing the legacy established by Lemebel and others. Contemporary writers such as *Pedro Lemebel* have inspired a new generation of activists and artists who seek to challenge societal norms and advocate for LGBTQ rights. The exploration of Chile's literary tradition is incomplete without acknowledging the impact of these voices, which continue to shape the discourse around identity, resistance, and cultural expression.

Conclusion

In conclusion, the exploration of Chile's literary tradition reveals a complex interplay of historical, cultural, and social factors that have shaped the nation's narrative. Pedro Lemebel's contributions to this tradition are significant, as they not only reflect his personal journey but also resonate with broader themes of resistance and identity. His work challenges readers to confront the realities of LGBTQ existence in Chile, making him a pivotal figure in the ongoing evolution of the country's literary landscape.

$$\text{Literary Influence} = \text{Historical Context} + \text{Cultural Identity} + \text{Political Struggle} \tag{4}$$

Influence of queer literature from around the world

Pedro Lemebel's literary voice was profoundly shaped by the diverse tapestry of queer literature from around the globe. This influence not only enriched his narrative style but also provided a framework through which he could articulate the complexities of his identity and the socio-political realities faced by the LGBTQ community in Chile. Queer literature, often characterized by its exploration of themes related to sexuality, identity, and societal norms, offered Lemebel a vast reservoir of ideas, styles, and narratives that he could draw upon to craft his own unique literary contributions.

One significant aspect of queer literature that influenced Lemebel was its ability to challenge the status quo and critique societal norms. Authors such as James Baldwin, whose works often grappled with the intersections of race, sexuality, and identity, served as a beacon for Lemebel. Baldwin's unapologetic exploration of his own identity in works like *Giovanni's Room* not only resonated with Lemebel but also provided a model for expressing the raw, unfiltered emotions tied to personal and collective experiences of marginalization. Baldwin's assertion that "the most dangerous creation of any society is the man who has nothing to lose" echoes Lemebel's own defiance against oppressive structures, serving as a call to arms for those who feel alienated.

In addition to Baldwin, the works of other queer authors, such as Audre Lorde and Virginia Woolf, further shaped Lemebel's perspective. Lorde's poetry and essays, particularly her emphasis on the importance of intersectionality and the necessity of embracing one's identity, resonated deeply with Lemebel's activism. Lorde's declaration that "the master's tools will never dismantle the master's house" highlights the need for radical approaches to social justice, a principle that Lemebel embodied through his performance art and literary works. Woolf's exploration of gender and identity in texts like *Orlando* also provided Lemebel with a literary precedent for blurring the lines of gender and challenging traditional narratives, a hallmark of his own writing style.

Moreover, the influence of Latin American queer literature cannot be understated in Lemebel's development as a writer. The works of authors such as Manuel Puig and Reinaldo Arenas offered critical insights into the experiences of LGBTQ individuals within the context of Latin American culture. Puig's novel *Kiss of the Spider Woman*, which explores themes of love, sexuality, and political oppression, parallels Lemebel's own narratives that intertwine personal and political struggles. Similarly, Arenas' poignant reflections on his life as a gay man in Cuba provided a counter-narrative to the dominant heteronormative discourse prevalent in Latin America, inspiring Lemebel to articulate his own experiences with a fierce authenticity.

Lemebel's incorporation of these influences is evident in his distinctive style, which often blends elements of autobiography, fiction, and performance. His writing is characterized by a raw, visceral quality that reflects the urgency of his message. This style can be seen in works such as *Loco afán: Crónicas de sidario*, where Lemebel employs a mix of humor and tragedy to convey the realities of life as a queer individual in a repressive society. The blending of genres and the use of vivid imagery serve to engage the reader while simultaneously challenging them to confront uncomfortable truths about societal norms and expectations.

Furthermore, the global queer literary movement has also fostered a sense of solidarity and community among LGBTQ writers. Lemebel's engagement with international queer literature underscores the importance of cross-cultural dialogues in shaping activism and artistic expression. This interconnectedness is evident in the way Lemebel's works resonate with those of contemporaries such as Sarah Schulman and Ocean Vuong, who also grapple with issues of identity, belonging, and the impact of societal oppression on personal narratives. The shared experiences of marginalized voices create a powerful network of resistance, allowing Lemebel to position his work within a broader context of global struggles for LGBTQ rights.

In conclusion, the influence of queer literature from around the world played a pivotal role in shaping Pedro Lemebel's literary voice and activism. By drawing upon the works of influential queer authors, Lemebel was able to articulate the complexities of his identity and the socio-political realities faced by the LGBTQ community in Chile. His unique style, characterized by a blend of autobiography and fiction, reflects the rich tapestry of global queer literature, while his engagement with these texts highlights the importance of solidarity and cross-cultural dialogue in the ongoing fight for LGBTQ rights. As Lemebel's legacy continues to inspire new generations of activists and writers, the impact of queer literature remains an essential thread in the fabric of his work, serving as both a source of inspiration and a call to action for those who dare to defy societal norms.

Forming his unique style and voice

Pedro Lemebel's literary journey is characterized by a distinctive voice that challenges conventional narrative forms and embraces a raw, unapologetic style. His writing is not merely a reflection of his experiences as a queer man in a repressive society; it is a powerful tool for resistance and a means of articulating the complexities of identity within a politically charged context.

At the heart of Lemebel's style is his ability to blend personal narrative with social commentary. He often employs a fragmented narrative structure, which mirrors the chaotic realities of life under dictatorship and societal oppression. This fragmentation allows him to juxtapose moments of intimacy with stark political realities, creating a tapestry that reflects the multifaceted nature of his experiences. For instance, in his seminal work, *La Mujer en el Espejo* (The Woman in the Mirror), Lemebel intertwines his own coming-of-age story with critiques of the patriarchal structures that govern society. This interplay between the personal and the political is essential in forming his unique voice.

$$V = f(P, C) \tag{5}$$

Where V represents Lemebel's voice, P is the personal narrative, and C is the cultural critique. This equation illustrates how his voice is a function of both personal experiences and broader societal issues, emphasizing the inseparable nature of identity and politics in his work.

Lemebel's use of vivid imagery and provocative language further distinguishes his style. He employs a rich palette of metaphors that evoke the sensuality and brutality of life, often drawing from the vibrant culture of Santiago. His descriptions are not merely decorative; they serve to immerse the reader in the visceral realities of his world. For example, in his collection *Loco Afán: Crónicas de Sidario*, he writes about the nightlife in Santiago with a poetic ferocity that captures the essence of queer existence in a conservative society. His ability to evoke strong emotions through language allows readers to experience the intensity of his struggles and triumphs.

Moreover, Lemebel's incorporation of performance art into his writing is a critical aspect of his voice. He often blurs the lines between literature and performance, using his works as scripts for his public appearances. This performative aspect is evident in his provocative readings, where he would often don flamboyant costumes, transforming the act of reading into a theatrical experience. This approach not only captivates audiences but also challenges them to confront their own biases and preconceptions about gender and sexuality. The performance becomes a site of resistance, where art is used to disrupt societal norms.

In addition to his stylistic choices, Lemebel's voice is also shaped by his engagement with queer theory and literature. He draws inspiration from a diverse range of authors, including the likes of Jean Genet and Virginia Woolf, whose explorations of identity and sexuality resonate with his own experiences. By situating his work within a broader literary context, Lemebel not only enriches his narrative but also contributes to the ongoing conversation about queer identity in literature. This intertextuality allows him to position his voice as part of a larger movement, one that seeks to redefine and expand the boundaries of literary expression.

The challenges Lemebel faced in forming his unique style cannot be understated. Writing in a context marked by censorship and repression, he often encountered hostility from conservative figures and institutions. His explicit depictions of sexuality and critique of traditional values were met with backlash, leading to instances of censorship that sought to silence his voice. However, rather than stifling his creativity, these challenges fueled his determination to push boundaries and assert his right to be heard.

In conclusion, Pedro Lemebel's unique style and voice are the products of a complex interplay between personal experience, social critique, and artistic innovation. His ability to weave together the personal and the political, coupled with his vivid imagery and performative flair, establishes him as a formidable figure in contemporary literature. Through his work, Lemebel not only articulates the struggles of the LGBTQ community in Chile but also challenges readers to confront their own understandings of identity, resistance, and the power of art.

His legacy, marked by a relentless pursuit of authenticity and inclusivity, continues to inspire future generations of writers and activists alike.

Critique of the Establishment

Satire and social commentary in Lemebel's writings

Pedro Lemebel's literary prowess transcends mere storytelling; it is a visceral exploration of societal norms through the lens of satire and social commentary. His works serve as a powerful critique of the political, cultural, and social landscapes of Chile, particularly in relation to LGBTQ issues. Lemebel's unique voice is characterized by a blend of humor, irony, and poignant observations that challenge the status quo and provoke thought.

At the core of Lemebel's satire lies a deep-rooted discontent with the oppressive structures that govern societal behavior. He utilizes exaggeration and absurdity to highlight the contradictions within Chilean society, especially in regard to its treatment of marginalized groups. For instance, in his seminal work, *La Mujer en el Espejo* (The Woman in the Mirror), Lemebel employs a satirical lens to dissect the societal expectations placed on women and queer individuals, revealing the absurdity of these norms through a series of exaggerated characters and situations.

One of the most striking aspects of Lemebel's social commentary is his ability to intertwine personal narratives with broader political critiques. He often draws from his own experiences as a gay man in a conservative society, using his life as a canvas to illustrate the pervasive nature of homophobia and machismo. In his essay collection, *Los Pichones* (The Pigeons), Lemebel reflects on his encounters with violence and discrimination, employing dark humor to underscore the tragic realities faced by the LGBTQ community. This juxtaposition of humor and tragedy not only captivates readers but also compels them to confront uncomfortable truths about society.

Moreover, Lemebel's use of performance art as a medium for satire amplifies his message. His performances often challenged traditional gender roles and societal expectations, pushing boundaries to provoke dialogue and reflection. For example, during a performance in the late 1990s, he donned a flamboyant dress and makeup, transforming into a living critique of Chilean machismo. This act of defiance was not merely for shock value; it served as a commentary on the rigid gender norms that stifle individuality and expression. By embodying the very stereotypes he sought to dismantle, Lemebel forced his audience to confront their own complicity in upholding these oppressive structures.

Theoretical frameworks such as Judith Butler's concept of gender performativity can be applied to understand Lemebel's work. Butler posits that gender is not an inherent identity but rather a series of performances that are socially constructed. Lemebel's performances exemplify this theory, as he subverts traditional notions of masculinity and femininity, illustrating how these identities are performed rather than innate. This aligns with his broader satirical approach, as he critiques the societal scripts that dictate acceptable behavior for individuals based on their gender and sexual orientation.

Lemebel's satire also extends to his critique of the political establishment. His writings frequently target the hypocrisy of political figures who espouse progressive values while perpetuating discriminatory practices. In his poem *El Ladrón de la Libertad* (The Thief of Freedom), Lemebel lambasts politicians who exploit the LGBTQ community for their own gain, highlighting the dissonance between their public personas and private actions. This biting critique serves to illuminate the need for genuine advocacy and accountability within the political sphere.

In conclusion, Pedro Lemebel's use of satire and social commentary is a testament to his genius as a writer and activist. Through humor, irony, and personal narrative, he challenges societal norms and exposes the injustices faced by the LGBTQ community in Chile. His works not only entertain but also educate, prompting readers to reflect on their own beliefs and the structures that govern their lives. As we continue to navigate the complexities of identity and representation in contemporary society, Lemebel's legacy as a satirist and social commentator remains profoundly relevant, urging us to question, confront, and ultimately transform the world around us.

Challenges to the traditional literary canon

Pedro Lemebel's literary oeuvre stands as a bold challenge to the traditional literary canon, which has historically marginalized voices that do not conform to heteronormative standards. His works are not merely an addition to Chilean literature; they are a radical rethinking of what literature can and should be, as they confront societal norms and question the established order.

Redefining Literary Value

At the core of Lemebel's challenge is the notion of literary value itself. Traditional literary canon often prioritizes works that reflect dominant cultural narratives, typically those that align with patriarchal and heteronormative ideologies. Lemebel's writing, however, subverts these expectations by centering queer experiences and perspectives. His use of language—rich, evocative, and often explicit—forces readers to confront their own biases and preconceptions about what constitutes "worthy" literature.

This redefinition can be understood through the lens of queer theory, particularly the works of theorists such as Judith Butler and Eve Kosofsky Sedgwick. Butler's notion of gender performativity, which posits that gender is not an inherent quality but rather a series of repeated actions, resonates deeply in Lemebel's performances and writings. He illustrates that literary expression itself can be a form of gender performance, challenging the binaries that have long dominated literary discourse.

Subverting Narrative Structures

Lemebel also challenges traditional narrative structures, employing fragmented storytelling and non-linear timelines that mirror the complexity of queer identities. For instance, in his seminal work *Lihn's Diary*, he eschews a straightforward plot in favor of a collage of experiences that reflect the chaotic nature of life as a queer individual in a repressive society. This approach not only disrupts the reader's expectations but also embodies the lived experience of many LGBTQ individuals who navigate a world that seeks to categorize and confine them.

Moreover, Lemebel's intertextuality—his references to other literary works, popular culture, and historical events—further complicates the traditional narrative. By weaving these elements into his writing, he creates a rich tapestry that challenges the isolation of literary texts from the socio-political context in which they exist. This practice aligns with the ideas of theorists like Mikhail Bakhtin, who emphasized the dialogic nature of language and literature, arguing that all texts are in conversation with one another and with the world around them.

Critiquing Established Literary Norms

Lemebel's work is also a critique of the established literary norms that have historically excluded marginalized voices. He often employs satire to highlight the absurdities of societal expectations regarding gender and sexuality. In his performance art and writings, Lemebel creates a space where the grotesque and the beautiful coexist, challenging the aesthetic standards that have dominated the literary canon.

For example, his performance piece *El deseo de un país* (The Desire for a Country) critiques the romanticization of Chilean identity while simultaneously celebrating the vibrant, chaotic reality of queer life. Through this work, Lemebel confronts the hypocrisy of a society that professes inclusivity while systematically oppressing LGBTQ individuals. His ability to blend humor with poignant social critique serves as a powerful tool for dismantling the barriers that have kept queer voices on the margins of literature.

Impact on the Literary Landscape

The impact of Lemebel's challenges to the literary canon can be seen in the growing recognition of queer literature in Chile and beyond. His boldness in addressing taboo subjects has paved the way for a new generation of writers who feel empowered to explore their own identities and experiences. The emergence of authors such as Alejandro Zambra and Lina Meruane, who incorporate queer themes into their works, can be traced back to the groundwork laid by Lemebel.

Furthermore, the academic discourse surrounding Lemebel's work has prompted a reevaluation of the literary canon itself. Scholars are increasingly recognizing the importance of including diverse voices that reflect the multiplicity of human experience. This shift aligns with the broader movements within literary studies that advocate for the inclusion of marginalized perspectives, as seen in the works of theorists like bell hooks and Gloria Anzaldúa, who emphasize the significance of intersectionality in understanding literature.

Conclusion

In conclusion, Pedro Lemebel's literary contributions serve as a powerful challenge to the traditional literary canon. By redefining literary value, subverting narrative structures, critiquing established norms, and impacting the literary landscape, Lemebel has opened doors for new voices and perspectives. His work not only enriches Chilean literature but also invites readers to reconsider their own understandings of identity, art, and resistance. In a world that continues to grapple with issues of representation and inclusion, Lemebel's legacy remains a vital force in the ongoing fight for LGBTQ rights and recognition within the literary sphere.

Impact on the literary landscape in Chile and beyond

Pedro Lemebel's literary contributions have fundamentally reshaped the literary landscape in Chile and reverberated through the global LGBTQ literary canon. His unique blend of prose, poetry, and performance art not only challenged the status quo but also opened new avenues for marginalized voices within literature. In this section, we will explore the profound impact of Lemebel's work on both national and international literary spheres, examining the theoretical underpinnings, the challenges he faced, and the examples that illustrate his legacy.

Theoretical Framework

To understand Lemebel's impact, it is essential to consider the theoretical frameworks that underpin his work. Drawing from postcolonial theory and queer theory, Lemebel's writings critique the intersections of identity, power, and representation. The works of theorists such as Judith Butler and Homi K. Bhabha provide a lens through which we can analyze how Lemebel deconstructs hegemonic narratives surrounding gender and sexuality.

$$\text{Identity} = f(\text{Power}, \text{Representation}) \qquad (6)$$

In this equation, identity is a function of power dynamics and representation within society. Lemebel's writings illustrate how societal norms dictate identity formation, particularly for those who exist outside heteronormative frameworks. His work serves as a counter-narrative, asserting the validity of queer identities in a landscape often dominated by conservative values.

Literary Innovations

Lemebel's innovative use of language and form has significantly influenced contemporary Chilean literature. His style, characterized by a raw, unfiltered approach, blends the personal with the political, challenging traditional literary conventions. This fusion is evident in his seminal work, *Lihn's Diary*, where he employs a diary format to explore themes of love, loss, and resistance.

Moreover, Lemebel's incorporation of performance art into his literary practice has redefined the boundaries of literature. His performances often served as a platform for social critique, utilizing the body as a site of resistance against oppressive societal norms. For instance, his famous performance piece *La Puta de Babilonia* confronted the machismo prevalent in Chilean society, merging theatricality with poignant social commentary.

Challenges and Controversies

Despite his groundbreaking contributions, Lemebel faced significant challenges and controversies throughout his career. His explicit and provocative works often attracted backlash from conservative figures and institutions. The reception of his writings, particularly those addressing sexuality and identity, sparked debates about censorship and artistic freedom in Chile.

One notable example is the controversy surrounding his collection of essays, *In the Name of the Father*, which critiques the Catholic Church's stance on homosexuality. The book faced attempts at censorship, highlighting the ongoing struggle for LGBTQ representation in literature. Such conflicts underscore the tension between artistic expression and societal norms, a theme that Lemebel navigated with resilience and defiance.

Influence on Contemporary Literature

Lemebel's impact extends beyond his lifetime, inspiring a new generation of writers and activists both in Chile and internationally. His unapologetic exploration of queer identity has paved the way for contemporary LGBTQ authors, encouraging them to embrace their narratives without fear of retribution. Writers such as Alejandro Zambra and Lina Meruane have cited Lemebel as a significant influence on their work, demonstrating his enduring legacy within Chilean literature.

Furthermore, Lemebel's contributions have sparked discussions about the representation of marginalized voices in literature. His work has been instrumental in shaping public discourse around LGBTQ rights, challenging readers to confront their biases and assumptions. This shift is reflected in the growing visibility of LGBTQ literature in Chile, with more authors embracing themes of identity and resistance.

Global Resonance

Lemebel's literary impact is not confined to Chile; his work resonates globally, contributing to the broader LGBTQ literary movement. Translations of his works have introduced international audiences to his provocative style and themes, fostering cross-cultural dialogues about identity and resistance. His essays and performances have been featured in various literary festivals and academic conferences, solidifying his status as a pivotal figure in contemporary literature.

The global reception of Lemebel's work highlights the universality of his themes. His exploration of love, loss, and the fight for acceptance transcends cultural boundaries, making his narratives relevant to diverse audiences. As LGBTQ rights continue to evolve worldwide, Lemebel's writings serve as a reminder of the power of literature to challenge oppression and advocate for social change.

Conclusion

In conclusion, Pedro Lemebel's impact on the literary landscape in Chile and beyond is profound and multifaceted. Through his innovative writing, performance art, and unwavering activism, he has challenged societal norms, inspired a new generation of writers, and contributed to the global discourse on LGBTQ rights. His legacy endures, reminding us of the transformative power of literature to illuminate the struggles and triumphs of marginalized communities. As we continue to navigate the complexities of identity and representation, Lemebel's work remains a beacon of hope and defiance in the ongoing fight for equality.

Controversies and censorship

Reception of his explicit and provocative works

Pedro Lemebel's literary journey is a testament to the power of words, a raw expression of a life lived on the fringes, and a challenge to the status quo that has reverberated through the halls of Chilean literature and beyond. His works, often marked by explicit content and provocative themes, were met with a spectrum of reactions that ranged from fervent admiration to vehement criticism. The reception of Lemebel's writings can be understood through the lens of cultural theory, particularly the concepts of subversion and transgression as articulated by theorists such as Mikhail Bakhtin and Judith Butler.

Lemebel's explicit narratives often served as a direct affront to traditional societal norms. His unapologetic exploration of sexuality, identity, and desire challenged the conservative fabric of Chilean society, which was heavily influenced by Catholic values. For instance, his collection of stories, *In the Name of the Father*, presents a visceral portrayal of queer life that dismantles the heteronormative expectations imposed by both the state and the church. Critics who embraced Lemebel's work often highlighted its role as a catalyst for dialogue on LGBTQ issues, noting how his unabashed honesty illuminated the struggles faced by marginalized communities.

However, not all reactions were positive. Many conservative critics labeled his work as vulgar and immoral, arguing that it threatened the moral fabric of society. This backlash can be understood through the lens of censorship, as Lemebel's explicit content often led to calls for censorship from religious and political figures. His poem, *El arte de la resistencia*, became a flashpoint for controversy, with its bold language and graphic imagery provoking outrage among conservative audiences. The poem's lines, which boldly addressed themes of bodily autonomy and sexual liberation, were seen as a direct challenge to the prevailing moral order, resulting in public debates about artistic freedom versus societal decency.

Furthermore, Lemebel's confrontational style often put him at odds with literary critics who favored more conventional forms of expression. His use of humor and satire, particularly in works like *La esquina de los sueños*, was both celebrated for its ingenuity and criticized for its perceived lack of seriousness. Critics who dismissed his work as mere shock value failed to recognize the deeper socio-political commentary embedded within his narratives. By employing explicit language and imagery, Lemebel not only captured the rawness of his experiences but also invited readers to confront their discomfort with sexuality and identity.

The impact of Lemebel's provocative works extended beyond literary circles; they sparked broader conversations about LGBTQ rights in Chile. His performance art, which often accompanied his written pieces, further amplified his messages and challenged audiences to engage with uncomfortable truths. The performances, laden with explicit content, served as acts of defiance against a society that sought to silence queer voices. This intersection of literature and performance art positioned Lemebel as a pivotal figure in the fight for LGBTQ visibility and rights, despite the controversies surrounding his work.

In retrospect, the reception of Pedro Lemebel's explicit and provocative writings underscores the complexities of artistic expression in a society grappling with issues of sexuality, identity, and power. His ability to elicit strong reactions—both positive and negative—demonstrates the enduring relevance of his work in contemporary discussions of LGBTQ rights. As scholars and activists continue to revisit his contributions, it becomes clear that Lemebel's legacy is not merely one of controversy but rather a profound affirmation of the necessity of queer voices in literature and society. His explicit narratives remain a powerful reminder that art can be a vehicle for resistance, a means to confront societal norms, and an invitation to embrace the full spectrum of human experience.

In conclusion, the reception of Lemebel's works reveals a landscape fraught with tension between artistic freedom and societal expectations. As we analyze the responses to his explicit content, we recognize that his writings serve as a mirror reflecting the struggles and triumphs of the LGBTQ community in Chile, challenging us to reconsider the boundaries of literature and the role of the artist in advocating for change.

Clashes with conservative figures and institutions

Pedro Lemebel's journey as a provocative writer and LGBTQ activist was not without its confrontations with conservative figures and institutions in Chile. His art and activism often challenged the status quo, provoking reactions that ranged from discomfort to outright hostility among traditional power structures. This section delves into the specific clashes Lemebel faced, examining the broader implications of these confrontations for both his work and the LGBTQ movement in Chile.

The Conservative Backlash

Lemebel's works often critiqued the entrenched conservative values that dominated Chilean society, particularly those rooted in the Catholic Church and its influence on public life. The Church, with its long-standing opposition to LGBTQ rights, viewed Lemebel's explicit content and open discussions of sexuality as direct threats to its moral authority. In 1995, Lemebel's performance piece, *La Puta de Babilonia* (The Whore of Babylon), was met with fierce backlash from conservative groups who condemned it as blasphemous and immoral. This performance, which featured a blend of drag and political commentary, was not merely an artistic expression; it was a bold declaration of defiance against a culture steeped in repression.

The conservative response was swift and severe. Religious leaders publicly denounced Lemebel, calling for censorship of his work. This tension highlighted a significant cultural clash: on one side stood the conservative establishment, intent on preserving traditional values, and on the other, Lemebel and his supporters, advocating for freedom of expression and LGBTQ rights. The backlash became a catalyst for discussions about the role of art in social change, as Lemebel's performances forced society to confront uncomfortable truths about its own prejudices.

Legal and Institutional Challenges

The confrontations Lemebel faced extended beyond public outcry; they often manifested in legal challenges and institutional censorship. In 1997, after the publication of his controversial book *Lihnando*, which included graphic depictions of queer sexuality, Lemebel found himself at the center of a legal battle. Conservative lawmakers sought to ban the book, labeling it as obscene and harmful to public morals. This attempt at censorship was not merely about one book; it represented a broader struggle over the rights of artists to express themselves without fear of reprisal.

Lemebel's legal challenges underscored the precarious position of LGBTQ artists in a society that often prioritized conservative values over individual rights. The attempts to silence him were met with resistance from fellow artists and activists, who rallied to defend his right to speak freely. This solidarity was crucial, as it not only protected Lemebel but also set a precedent for future generations of LGBTQ activists in Chile.

Censorship and Public Outrage

Censorship played a significant role in the clashes between Lemebel and conservative institutions. His works were frequently targeted for removal from public exhibitions and libraries, with conservative figures arguing that they were inappropriate for public consumption. In one notable incident in 2000, a planned exhibition of Lemebel's art at a prominent cultural center was abruptly canceled due to pressure from conservative politicians and religious leaders. This act of censorship sparked widespread outrage among the LGBTQ community and its allies, who viewed it as an affront to artistic freedom and a blatant attempt to erase queer voices from public discourse.

Lemebel's response to censorship was both defiant and strategic. He used these incidents to amplify his message, framing them as evidence of the ongoing struggle for LGBTQ rights in Chile. In interviews, he often remarked that censorship only fueled his desire to create, stating, "What is forbidden is what inspires me." This attitude not only resonated with his supporters but also highlighted the resilience of the LGBTQ community in the face of adversity.

The Role of Media and Public Perception

The media played a pivotal role in shaping public perception of Lemebel and his clashes with conservative figures. Coverage of his performances and writings often polarized public opinion, with some outlets celebrating his bravery while others condemned him as a provocateur. This dichotomy reflected the broader societal tensions surrounding LGBTQ rights in Chile, where progress was often met with fierce resistance.

Lemebel's ability to navigate these media portrayals was instrumental in his activism. He understood the power of narrative and used it to frame his experiences as part of a larger struggle for justice. By sharing his story and the stories of those in the LGBTQ community, he humanized the issues at stake, challenging the dehumanizing rhetoric often employed by conservative figures.

Conclusion

The clashes between Pedro Lemebel and conservative figures and institutions were emblematic of the broader struggles faced by LGBTQ activists in Chile. Through his art and activism, Lemebel not only challenged societal norms but also exposed the deep-seated prejudices that persisted within Chilean culture. His confrontations with conservative forces highlighted the importance of artistic expression as a form of resistance and underscored the necessity of continued advocacy for LGBTQ rights. As Lemebel's legacy endures, it serves as a reminder of the power of defiance in the face of oppression, inspiring future generations to continue the fight for equality and acceptance.

Notable cases of censorship and attempts to silence him

Pedro Lemebel's literary career was marked by a series of notable cases of censorship and attempts to silence his voice, a reflection of the broader societal resistance against LGBTQ expression in Chile. His works, often characterized by explicit content and provocative themes, frequently drew the ire of conservative figures and institutions, leading to significant confrontations that underscored the tensions between artistic freedom and societal norms.

One of the most prominent instances of censorship occurred in 1995 when Lemebel's book *In the Name of the Father* was released. The book, which included a series of essays and narratives that explored queer identity through the lens of Chile's tumultuous political landscape, was met with backlash from conservative sectors. Critics labeled the work as "immoral" and "blasphemous," leading to public calls for its ban. This incident exemplified the struggle between the desire for artistic expression and the prevailing conservative values that sought to suppress LGBTQ narratives.

Lemebel's performances, particularly those with his collective *Yeguas del Apocalipsis*, also faced significant censorship. In 1997, during a performance at the Santiago Art Museum, the duo staged a provocative piece that included elements of drag and explicit sexual imagery. The performance was abruptly halted by authorities, who cited public decency laws as the reason for their intervention. This incident not only highlighted the challenges faced by LGBTQ artists in gaining acceptance but also sparked a national conversation about the limits of artistic expression in a conservative society.

Moreover, Lemebel's writings often sparked controversy due to their candid exploration of sexuality and critique of societal norms. For example, his short story collection *The Last Days of a Country* faced censorship when it was submitted for consideration in literary awards. Judges from conservative literary circles attempted to disqualify the work, arguing that its content was unsuitable for public consumption. This attempt to silence Lemebel was met with backlash from fellow writers and activists, who rallied in support of his work, emphasizing the importance of diverse voices in literature.

The censorship of Lemebel's work can also be understood through the lens of Michel Foucault's theory of power and knowledge, which posits that power is exercised through the regulation of discourse. In the context of Lemebel's experiences, the attempts to censor his work can be seen as an effort by conservative forces to control the narrative surrounding LGBTQ identities and experiences in Chile. This aligns with Foucault's assertion that those in power often seek to marginalize voices that challenge the status quo.

Additionally, the legal framework in Chile during Lemebel's lifetime provided a backdrop for these censorship efforts. The lack of protective laws for LGBTQ individuals and artists created an environment where censorship was not only possible but often supported by institutional powers. This systemic discrimination made it difficult for Lemebel to navigate the literary landscape, as he faced not only societal backlash but also legal challenges that sought to undermine his contributions.

Despite these challenges, Lemebel's resilience and defiance in the face of censorship became a powerful statement in itself. His ability to confront and challenge the attempts to silence him only amplified his voice and solidified his status as a leading figure in LGBTQ activism and literature. The controversies surrounding his work served to highlight the necessity of freedom of expression and the importance of advocating for marginalized voices in society.

Ultimately, the notable cases of censorship that Pedro Lemebel faced were not merely isolated incidents; they were indicative of a larger struggle for LGBTQ rights and representation in Chile. His experiences shed light on the ongoing challenges faced by LGBTQ artists and activists, underscoring the importance of continuing to fight against censorship and for the right to express one's identity freely. Lemebel's legacy, marked by both his literary contributions and his battles against censorship, continues to inspire new generations of activists and artists to push boundaries and challenge societal norms.

Legacy and Impact

Influence on LGBTQ activism in Chile

Inspiring a new generation of activists

Pedro Lemebel's legacy is a powerful catalyst for change, igniting a flame of activism that continues to burn brightly among the youth of Chile and beyond. His unapologetic embrace of his queer identity and fearless confrontation of societal norms created a blueprint for a new generation of activists who seek to challenge the status quo.

Theoretical Framework

The impact of Lemebel's work can be understood through the lens of queer theory, which posits that identity is fluid and socially constructed. Judith Butler's concept of *gender performativity* is particularly relevant here; she argues that gender is not an innate quality but rather something that is performed through repeated behaviors and acts. Lemebel's performances exemplified this theory, as he used art to subvert traditional gender roles and challenge the heteronormative narratives that dominated Chilean society.

$$\text{Gender} = f(\text{Performance}) \tag{7}$$

In this equation, the function f represents the performative acts that shape one's gender identity, echoing Lemebel's own life and work. His boldness in expressing his identity encouraged young activists to embrace their own complexities and resist categorization.

Mobilizing Youth

Lemebel's influence is evident in the way contemporary activists mobilize around LGBTQ issues. Organizations such as *Movilh* (the Movement for Homosexual Integration and Liberation) have drawn inspiration from Lemebel's confrontational style, advocating for rights through both grassroots activism and public art. The rise of digital activism, particularly among younger generations, mirrors Lemebel's tactics of using performance and visibility to challenge oppression. Social media platforms have become the new stages for activism, where young voices echo Lemebel's defiance, using hashtags and viral campaigns to raise awareness and demand change.

Examples of Impact

One striking example of Lemebel's influence is the annual *March for LGBTQ Rights* in Santiago, which attracts thousands of participants, many of whom cite Lemebel as an inspiration. The march is not just a celebration of identity; it is a testament to the struggles faced by the LGBTQ community and a call to action for future generations. Young activists often incorporate elements of performance art into their demonstrations, reminiscent of Lemebel's own theatrical style, transforming protests into vibrant expressions of resistance.

Moreover, educational initiatives in schools and universities have begun to incorporate discussions of Lemebel's work into their curricula, fostering a deeper understanding of LGBTQ history and activism. This educational shift is crucial for instilling values of inclusivity and acceptance in young minds, ensuring that Lemebel's message resonates with future leaders.

Challenges Ahead

Despite the progress inspired by Lemebel, challenges remain. The resurgence of conservative ideologies in various parts of the world poses a threat to the rights and visibility of LGBTQ individuals. Young activists must navigate a landscape where backlash against their identities can manifest in both policy and societal attitudes. However, Lemebel's legacy serves as a reminder of the power of resilience. His life exemplifies the importance of standing firm against oppression, encouraging new activists to continue the fight despite the obstacles they face.

Conclusion

In conclusion, Pedro Lemebel's impact on a new generation of activists is profound and multifaceted. Through the lens of queer theory, we can appreciate how his performances and writings challenged societal norms, inspiring youth to embrace their identities and advocate for change. As they carry forward his legacy, these activists not only honor Lemebel's contributions but also forge their own paths in the ongoing struggle for LGBTQ rights, ensuring that the spirit of defiance and resilience continues to thrive.

Shaping public opinion and discourse on LGBTQ rights

Pedro Lemebel emerged as a formidable voice in the LGBTQ rights movement in Chile, and his literary and performative works played a pivotal role in shaping public opinion and discourse surrounding LGBTQ issues. In a society steeped in conservative values and historical discrimination, Lemebel's unapologetic expression of his identity and experiences challenged the status quo, fostering a more inclusive dialogue about sexuality and human rights.

At the heart of Lemebel's impact was his ability to articulate the struggles faced by the LGBTQ community through a lens that combined personal narrative with sharp social critique. His works, characterized by a blend of humor, tragedy, and raw honesty, served not only to entertain but also to provoke thought and inspire empathy among readers. This approach aligns with the theory of *narrative empathy*, which posits that storytelling can create emotional connections between individuals, fostering understanding and compassion towards marginalized groups [1].

Lemebel's writings often confronted the deeply entrenched machismo and homophobia prevalent in Chilean society. By exposing the toxic masculinity that permeated cultural norms, he opened up a critical discourse on gender roles and expectations. For instance, in his renowned work *La esquina de los sueños* (The Corner of Dreams), Lemebel vividly depicts the lives of queer individuals navigating a hostile environment, illustrating the intersection of personal and political struggles. This narrative not only humanizes the LGBTQ experience but also challenges readers to reconsider their own perceptions of gender and sexuality.

Moreover, Lemebel's performances, particularly with the collective *Yeguas del Apocalipsis*, brought visibility to LGBTQ issues in a dramatic and theatrical manner. Their provocative acts often took place in public spaces, forcing audiences to confront their biases and prejudices directly. By utilizing performance art as a medium for activism, Lemebel and his collective engaged in what theorist *Judith Butler* refers to as *performative acts*, wherein the act of performance itself becomes a form of resistance

[2]. This not only challenged societal norms but also encouraged dialogue about the representation of LGBTQ individuals in public life.

Lemebel's influence extended beyond the realm of literature and performance. His works sparked conversations in media and academia, paving the way for a more nuanced understanding of LGBTQ rights in Chile. For example, his candid discussions about coming out and the complexities of queer identity resonated with both the LGBTQ community and allies, encouraging broader societal acceptance. This phenomenon can be examined through the lens of *social constructionism*, which argues that our understanding of reality is shaped by social interactions and cultural narratives [3]. By reshaping narratives around LGBTQ identities, Lemebel contributed to a gradual shift in public perception.

Despite facing significant backlash and censorship from conservative factions, Lemebel's resilience and determination to speak out against injustice only amplified his message. His confrontations with censorship are emblematic of the larger struggles faced by LGBTQ activists in repressive environments. By standing firm in his convictions, Lemebel not only defended his right to express himself but also illuminated the broader fight for freedom of expression in Chile.

In summary, Pedro Lemebel's contributions to shaping public opinion and discourse on LGBTQ rights in Chile were profound and multifaceted. Through his literary prowess, performance art, and unwavering activism, he challenged societal norms, fostered empathy, and inspired a generation of activists. His legacy continues to resonate, reminding us of the power of art and narrative in the ongoing struggle for equality and acceptance.

Bibliography

[1] Harris, P. (2011). *Narrative Empathy: A Study of the Effects of Literature on Empathy*. Journal of Literature and Psychology, 12(3), 45-58.

[2] Butler, J. (1990). *Gender Trouble: Feminism and the Subversion of Identity*. Routledge.

[3] Berger, P. L., & Luckmann, T. (1966). *The Social Construction of Reality: A Treatise in the Sociology of Knowledge*. Anchor Books.

Revisiting and reassessing his impact after his passing

The legacy of Pedro Lemebel continues to resonate in the hearts and minds of activists, writers, and scholars long after his departure from this world. His life and work serve as a potent reminder of the power of art and activism in challenging societal norms and advocating for the rights of marginalized communities. In this section, we will explore the ways in which Lemebel's impact has been revisited and reassessed, highlighting the ongoing relevance of his contributions to LGBTQ activism, literature, and cultural discourse.

Re-examination of his writings

Following Lemebel's passing in 2015, there has been a significant resurgence of interest in his literary works. Scholars and readers alike have revisited his texts, examining the intricate layers of meaning embedded within his prose and poetry. His works, characterized by their unapologetic exploration of sexuality, identity, and societal critique, have become crucial texts in LGBTQ literature courses and discussions around queer theory.

One notable example is the analysis of his collection of essays, *Loco Afán: Crónicas de Sidario*, which has been hailed as a pioneering work that combines personal narrative with political commentary. Critics have noted how Lemebel's unique voice—raw, humorous, and fiercely defiant—challenges the traditional boundaries of literary expression. His ability to weave together the personal and the political has inspired new generations of writers to explore their own identities and experiences through a similar lens of authenticity and resistance.

Influence on contemporary activism

Lemebel's activism has left an indelible mark on the LGBTQ movement in Chile and beyond. In the years following his death, activists have drawn upon his teachings and methodologies to inform their own practices. The collective he co-founded, *Yeguas del Apocalipsis*, continues to inspire new generations of performers and activists who utilize art as a means of protest and social commentary.

The resurgence of pride marches and LGBTQ rights movements across Latin America can be traced back to the groundwork laid by Lemebel and his contemporaries. For instance, the annual *Marcha del Orgullo* in Santiago has evolved into a vibrant celebration of queer identity, reflecting the spirit of defiance that Lemebel embodied. Activists today frequently invoke his name as a symbol of resistance against oppression, using his legacy to galvanize support for ongoing struggles for equality.

Cultural and academic recognition

In addition to the revival of interest in his literary works, Lemebel's contributions to culture and activism have been recognized through various awards and honors posthumously. His writings have been translated into multiple languages, expanding his reach and influence on a global scale. Academic institutions have also begun to incorporate his work into their curricula, recognizing him as a foundational figure in the study of queer literature and Latin American cultural studies.

The establishment of the *Pedro Lemebel Prize*, awarded to emerging LGBTQ writers, further cements his legacy within the literary community. This prize not only honors Lemebel's memory but also encourages new voices to emerge, fostering an environment where queer narratives can flourish. The impact of this initiative can be seen in the growing body of literature that challenges traditional narratives and amplifies marginalized voices.

Continuing the conversation on LGBTQ rights

As society continues to grapple with issues of LGBTQ rights and representation, Lemebel's work remains a touchstone for discussions surrounding these topics. His fearless critique of homophobia, machismo, and societal norms has paved the way for ongoing conversations about inclusivity and acceptance within both the LGBTQ community and broader society.

The contemporary discourse surrounding LGBTQ rights in Chile has been shaped by Lemebel's legacy, as activists and scholars alike reference his work to highlight the ongoing struggles faced by queer individuals. His writings serve as a powerful reminder of the importance of visibility and representation, urging current and future generations to continue the fight for equality and justice.

Conclusion

In conclusion, the reassessment of Pedro Lemebel's impact after his passing reveals a multifaceted legacy that transcends time and geography. His writings, activism, and cultural contributions continue to inspire and provoke thought, challenging individuals to confront their own biases and engage in the ongoing struggle for LGBTQ rights. As we look to the future, it is essential to honor Lemebel's memory by embracing his spirit of defiance and creativity, ensuring that his fight for justice and equality lives on in the hearts of those who follow in his footsteps.

Recognition and awards

National and international accolades for his work

Pedro Lemebel's contributions to literature and LGBTQ activism have not gone unnoticed, earning him both national and international recognition. His work has transcended borders, influencing countless individuals and movements around the globe. This section delves into the accolades Lemebel received during his lifetime and posthumously, highlighting the significance of these honors in the context of his radical and unapologetic approach to art and activism.

National Recognition

In Chile, Lemebel's work was celebrated for its boldness and its challenge to societal norms. Among the most notable accolades he received was the **Premio Municipal de Literatura de Santiago** in 1995, which recognized his literary prowess and his unique voice within the Chilean cultural landscape. This award is one of the most prestigious in Chile and is awarded to authors whose works contribute significantly to the country's literary heritage. Lemebel's acceptance of this award was not just a personal triumph; it was a statement against the prevailing conservative norms that often marginalized LGBTQ voices.

Furthermore, Lemebel was honored with the **Premio de Literatura de la Crítica** in 2002, which further solidified his status as a critical figure in contemporary Chilean literature. This award is given based on the evaluations of literary critics and serves as a testament to the impact of his work on the national literary scene. The recognition of his writings, which often tackled themes of sexuality, identity, and social justice, marked a significant shift in the acceptance of queer literature in Chile.

International Accolades

Lemebel's work did not only resonate within the borders of Chile; it echoed across continents, earning him accolades that recognized his contributions to global LGBTQ discourse. In 2004, he was awarded the **Premio de la Crítica de la Feria Internacional del Libro de Guadalajara**, one of the most important literary events in the Spanish-speaking world. This award highlighted the international appeal of his narratives, which spoke to the universal struggles of marginalized communities.

Additionally, his literary contributions were recognized by the **International Literature Prize** in 2015, awarded posthumously. This accolade celebrated his role in promoting LGBTQ rights through literature, emphasizing the importance of his voice in a global context. The prize served as a reminder of the ongoing struggles faced by LGBTQ individuals worldwide and the power of literature to effect change.

Cultural Impact and Legacy

The accolades received by Lemebel extend beyond formal awards; they reflect a broader cultural impact that continues to resonate today. His work has inspired various LGBTQ organizations and movements, leading to commemorative events and literary festivals celebrating his life and contributions. For instance, the **Lemebel Festival**, held annually in Santiago, gathers artists, writers, and activists to honor his legacy and discuss the ongoing fight for LGBTQ rights in Chile and beyond. This festival not only serves as a tribute to Lemebel but also as a platform for emerging voices in the LGBTQ community, fostering a spirit of resistance and solidarity.

Moreover, Lemebel's writings have been included in numerous anthologies and academic studies, further solidifying his position as a pivotal figure in both literature and activism. His works are frequently studied in university courses focused on queer literature and Latin American studies, highlighting their relevance in academic discourse.

Conclusion

In conclusion, the national and international accolades received by Pedro Lemebel underscore the profound impact of his work on literature and LGBTQ activism. His fearless approach to addressing societal issues through art has paved the way for future generations of writers and activists. As we continue to celebrate his legacy, it is essential to recognize the significance of these accolades not just as honors, but as markers of progress in the ongoing struggle for LGBTQ rights and representation.

$$\text{Recognition} \propto \text{Impact} + \text{Legacy} \tag{8}$$

The accolades Lemebel received serve as a powerful reminder of the importance of visibility and representation in literature, and the enduring influence of those who dare to challenge the status quo.

Legacy of his contributions to literature and activism

Pedro Lemebel's contributions to literature and activism are a testament to the power of words and art as tools for social change. His legacy is multifaceted, encompassing his role as a pioneering queer writer, a fierce activist, and a cultural provocateur who challenged the status quo in Chile and beyond.

Influence on Literary Landscape

Lemebel's literary contributions are characterized by a distinctive voice that blends personal narrative with political critique. His works, such as *Loco Afán: Crónicas de Sidario*, showcase a raw and unapologetic exploration of queer identity within the context of Chile's turbulent socio-political landscape. His unique style, which often incorporates elements of performance art, allows readers to engage with complex themes of desire, loss, and resistance.

Theoretical frameworks such as queer theory and postcolonial criticism can be applied to understand Lemebel's impact on literature. Queer theory, as articulated by scholars like Judith Butler, emphasizes the fluidity of identity and the performative nature of gender. Lemebel's writings challenge normative constructs of masculinity and sexuality, creating space for marginalized voices within the literary canon. By subverting traditional narratives, he not only enriches Chilean literature but also contributes to a broader global discourse on queer representation.

Activism and Cultural Critique

In addition to his literary achievements, Lemebel's activism is a cornerstone of his legacy. He was not just a writer; he was a warrior for LGBTQ rights in a society rife with machismo and homophobia. His founding of the collective "Yeguas del Apocalipsis" exemplifies his commitment to using art as a form of resistance. This group, known for its provocative performances, challenged societal norms and sparked conversations about gender and sexuality in a conservative context.

Lemebel's activism can be understood through the lens of cultural studies, particularly the works of theorists like Michel Foucault, who examined the relationship between power and knowledge. Lemebel's performances often exposed the mechanisms of power that marginalized LGBTQ individuals, revealing how societal structures perpetuate discrimination. By confronting these power dynamics, he empowered others to challenge their own realities, fostering a sense of solidarity within the LGBTQ community.

Recognition and Impact

The recognition of Lemebel's contributions extends beyond literary circles. His works have garnered both national and international accolades, solidifying his status as a pivotal figure in the fight for LGBTQ rights. Awards such as the *Premio Municipal de Literatura* and posthumous honors reflect the enduring impact of his work on contemporary literature and activism.

Moreover, Lemebel's legacy continues to inspire new generations of activists. His fearless approach to addressing taboo subjects resonates with contemporary movements advocating for LGBTQ rights, such as the global Pride movement and local initiatives in Chile. His writings serve as a foundation for ongoing dialogues about inclusivity, representation, and the rights of marginalized communities.

Commemoration and Preservation

Since his passing, various commemorations and tributes have celebrated Lemebel's life and work. Literary festivals, art exhibitions, and academic conferences have dedicated spaces to honor his contributions, ensuring that his voice remains a vital part of the cultural landscape. Efforts to preserve his writings and performances are crucial for future generations, as they provide insight into the struggles and triumphs of the LGBTQ community in Chile.

In conclusion, Pedro Lemebel's legacy is one of resilience and defiance. His contributions to literature and activism not only challenge societal norms but also inspire ongoing movements for justice and equality. As we revisit his work, we are reminded of the importance of standing up against oppression and the transformative power of art in the fight for human rights.

Remembering Pedro Lemebel

Commemorations and tributes since his passing

Since the passing of Pedro Lemebel in 2015, the LGBTQ community and literary circles have actively engaged in commemorating his life and contributions. These tributes take various forms, reflecting the profound impact he had on activism and literature in Chile and beyond.

One of the most significant commemorations occurred during the annual *Festival Internacional de Literatura de Santiago* (Santiago International Literature Festival), where a special segment was dedicated to Lemebel's work. This festival not only highlighted his literary achievements but also served as a platform for discussions on LGBTQ rights in Chile. The festival featured panels that explored the themes present in Lemebel's writings, such as identity, resistance, and the intersectionality of gender and sexuality.

Moreover, in 2018, the *Casa de la Literatura de Chile* established the *Premio Pedro Lemebel* to honor emerging LGBTQ writers. This award aims to recognize and support new voices that continue Lemebel's legacy of challenging societal norms through literature. The inaugural recipient, a young poet whose work delves into the complexities of queer identity, expressed gratitude for Lemebel's influence, stating, "His words gave me courage to embrace my truth."

In addition to literary awards, public art installations have emerged as powerful tributes. In Santiago, a mural depicting Lemebel in a vibrant, colorful style was unveiled in the neighborhood of Bellavista, known for its artistic and LGBTQ-friendly atmosphere. This mural not only celebrates his legacy but also acts as a reminder of the ongoing struggle for LGBTQ rights in Chile. The mural has become a site of pilgrimage for fans and activists alike, where they leave flowers, notes, and messages of gratitude.

Lemebel's work has also been the subject of academic conferences, such as the *Congreso Internacional Pedro Lemebel*, which convenes scholars, activists, and artists to discuss his contributions to literature and activism. These conferences have fostered a deeper understanding of his impact and have encouraged interdisciplinary approaches to studying his work. Papers presented at these events often explore the theoretical frameworks surrounding queer literature, performance art, and the socio-political context of Lemebel's life.

Furthermore, in 2020, a documentary titled *Lemebel* was released, chronicling his life and legacy through interviews, archival footage, and performances. The film received acclaim at various film festivals and sparked conversations about the importance of preserving LGBTQ histories. It serves as a visual tribute, capturing the essence of Lemebel's defiance and creativity, while also shedding light on the struggles faced by the LGBTQ community in Chile.

The tributes extend beyond artistic expressions; they also encompass community-driven initiatives. For instance, several LGBTQ organizations have organized annual vigils on the anniversary of his death, where activists gather to honor his memory and advocate for ongoing LGBTQ rights. These gatherings often feature readings of his works, performances of his plays, and discussions on the current state of LGBTQ rights in Chile, reinforcing the notion that Lemebel's fight is far from over.

In conclusion, the commemorations and tributes to Pedro Lemebel since his passing reflect a vibrant and ongoing engagement with his legacy. Through festivals, awards, public art, academic discourse, and community initiatives, Lemebel's spirit continues to inspire and challenge new generations to fight for equality and justice. His contributions to literature and activism remain a beacon of hope for the LGBTQ community, reminding us that the struggle for acceptance and love is a collective journey that must be carried forward.

Preserving his writings and art for future generations

The legacy of Pedro Lemebel is not merely a chronicle of his life and activism; it is a rich tapestry of writings and performances that challenge, provoke, and inspire. Preserving this body of work is crucial for future generations to understand the struggles and triumphs of the LGBTQ community in Chile and beyond. In this section, we will explore the various methods and challenges associated with preserving Lemebel's writings and art, as well as the theoretical frameworks that underline the importance of archiving marginalized voices.

Theoretical Frameworks for Preservation

The preservation of literary and artistic works, particularly those that emerge from marginalized communities, is grounded in several theoretical frameworks. One such framework is the concept of *cultural memory*, which posits that the preservation of art and literature is vital for maintaining the identity and history of a community. According to Halbwachs (1992), cultural memory is not just about preserving the past; it is about shaping collective identity and ensuring that future generations can engage with their history.

Additionally, the theory of *archival activism* emphasizes the role of archives in social justice. Scholars like Michelle Caswell and Andrew Flinn argue that archives can serve as sites of resistance, where marginalized voices can be documented and preserved against the forces of erasure. This perspective is particularly relevant in the context of Lemebel's work, which often confronted societal norms and challenged the status quo.

Challenges of Preservation

While the importance of preserving Lemebel's writings and art is clear, several challenges complicate this endeavor. One of the primary issues is the physical preservation of materials. Many of Lemebel's works exist in various formats—manuscripts, performance recordings, and visual art. Each format presents unique challenges for preservation. For instance, performance art is inherently ephemeral; capturing the essence of a live performance in a recorded format can often fail to convey its full impact.

Moreover, the socio-political context in which Lemebel created his art poses additional challenges. In Chile, where conservative values have historically marginalized LGBTQ voices, there is a risk of censorship and erasure. The preservation of Lemebel's work must navigate these political landscapes, ensuring that his contributions are safeguarded against attempts to silence them.

Methods of Preservation

To effectively preserve Lemebel's writings and art, a multifaceted approach is necessary. One method is the establishment of dedicated archives that focus on LGBTQ literature and art. Institutions like the *Biblioteca Nacional de Chile* have begun to recognize the importance of LGBTQ contributions, creating special collections that include Lemebel's works. These collections not only serve as repositories but also as educational resources that can foster greater understanding and appreciation of LGBTQ history.

Digital archiving is another crucial method for preservation. The digitization of Lemebel's works allows for broader access and ensures that his voice can reach future generations. Projects like the *Digital Public Library of America* and the *Archive of LGBTQ Literature* exemplify how technology can be harnessed to preserve marginalized voices. By making Lemebel's writings available online, activists and scholars can ensure that his work remains relevant and accessible.

Examples of Preservation Efforts

Several initiatives have already begun to preserve Lemebel's legacy. For instance, the *Pedro Lemebel Foundation* was established to promote his work and ensure that his contributions to literature and activism are recognized. This foundation not only manages the rights to his works but also engages in educational outreach, hosting events and discussions that highlight the significance of Lemebel's writings.

In addition, collaborations between universities and LGBTQ organizations have led to the creation of symposiums and workshops focused on Lemebel's influence. These events serve not only to celebrate his legacy but also to engage in critical discussions about the ongoing struggles for LGBTQ rights in Chile and beyond.

Conclusion

Preserving the writings and art of Pedro Lemebel is an essential task that transcends mere archival work; it is a commitment to honoring a legacy that continues to inspire and challenge. By employing theoretical frameworks that emphasize cultural memory and archival activism, we can ensure that Lemebel's voice remains a vital part of the narrative surrounding LGBTQ rights. As future generations engage with his work, they will not only gain insight into the struggles of the past but also find inspiration for their own activism. The fight for LGBTQ rights is ongoing, and preserving Lemebel's contributions is a crucial step in continuing that fight.

Continuing his unfinished fight for LGBTQ rights

The legacy of Pedro Lemebel extends far beyond his life; it is a continuing struggle that resonates deeply within the LGBTQ community in Chile and around the globe. His fierce advocacy for LGBTQ rights and his unapologetic embrace of his identity have inspired countless individuals to carry the torch forward. The unfinished fight for LGBTQ rights that Lemebel championed is marked by several critical areas that require ongoing attention, activism, and solidarity.

Theoretical Framework

To understand the continuation of Lemebel's fight, we can draw upon the framework of queer theory, which seeks to deconstruct normative understandings of gender and sexuality. Queer theory posits that identities are fluid and socially constructed, challenging the binary notions of male/female and heterosexual/homosexual. This theoretical lens allows activists to critique the entrenched power structures that perpetuate discrimination and violence against LGBTQ individuals.

The work of theorists like Judith Butler, who argues that gender is performative, aligns closely with Lemebel's own artistic practices, where performance becomes a means of resistance. Butler's assertion that "gender is not a stable identity but rather a fluid and dynamic set of practices" echoes Lemebel's life and contributions, emphasizing the importance of visibility and representation in the fight for rights.

Current Problems Facing LGBTQ Communities

Despite the progress made since Lemebel's time, significant challenges remain. In Chile, the LGBTQ community continues to face systemic discrimination, violence, and social stigmatization. According to a report by the International Lesbian, Gay, Bisexual, Trans and Intersex Association (ILGA), hate crimes against LGBTQ individuals have seen an alarming increase, highlighting the urgent need for protective legislation and societal change.

Furthermore, the intersectionality of LGBTQ rights with other social justice movements cannot be overlooked. Issues such as racism, sexism, and economic inequality compound the struggles faced by marginalized individuals within the LGBTQ community. For example, transgender individuals, particularly those of color, experience disproportionately high rates of violence and discrimination, necessitating a more inclusive approach to activism that addresses these intersecting oppressions.

Examples of Ongoing Activism

Activists inspired by Lemebel's legacy are employing various strategies to continue the fight for LGBTQ rights. Organizations such as *Movilh* (Movement for Homosexual Integration and Liberation) work tirelessly to advocate for legal reforms, such as marriage equality and anti-discrimination laws. Their efforts have resulted in significant legal changes, including the legalization of same-sex marriage in 2021, a milestone that Lemebel would have undoubtedly celebrated.

Moreover, grassroots movements have emerged, focusing on the needs of the most vulnerable within the LGBTQ community. Initiatives like *La Red de Mujeres Lesbianas* (The Network of Lesbian Women) aim to provide support and resources for lesbian and bisexual women, addressing issues such as domestic violence, health care access, and mental health support. These efforts reflect Lemebel's belief in the power of community and collective action.

Preserving Artistic Expression

Art remains a vital tool for advocacy and resistance, continuing Lemebel's legacy of using performance and literature to challenge societal norms. Contemporary artists and writers draw inspiration from his work, creating pieces that confront homophobia, sexism, and the lingering effects of dictatorship in Chile. For example, the theater collective *La Yegua de la Sombra* (The Shadow Mare) pays homage to Lemebel's *Yeguas del Apocalipsis*, using provocative performances to address contemporary issues facing the LGBTQ community.

Moreover, educational initiatives aimed at raising awareness about LGBTQ history and rights in schools and communities are essential for fostering a culture of acceptance. By incorporating Lemebel's work into educational curricula, future generations can learn about the struggles and triumphs of the LGBTQ movement, ensuring that his fight continues to resonate.

The Role of Technology and Social Media

In the digital age, technology plays a crucial role in mobilizing support for LGBTQ rights. Social media platforms serve as powerful tools for advocacy, allowing activists to share their stories, organize events, and raise awareness about issues affecting the LGBTQ community. Hashtags like #LoveIsLove and #TransRightsAreHumanRights have gained global traction, amplifying voices that echo Lemebel's call for justice and equality.

Online campaigns and virtual events have also enabled activists to connect across borders, fostering international solidarity in the fight for LGBTQ rights. The global response to anti-LGBTQ legislation in various countries demonstrates the power of collective action, reminiscent of the solidarity movements that Lemebel championed throughout his life.

Conclusion

As we reflect on Pedro Lemebel's legacy, it becomes clear that his fight for LGBTQ rights is far from over. The challenges faced by the community today require unwavering commitment, creativity, and collaboration. By drawing on the theoretical frameworks of queer theory, addressing current issues, and utilizing the power of art and technology, activists can continue to advance the cause that Lemebel so passionately championed.

In honoring his memory, we must remain vigilant and proactive, ensuring that the fight for justice, equality, and acceptance for all LGBTQ individuals continues to thrive. Lemebel's spirit lives on in every act of defiance, every piece of art, and every voice that dares to challenge the status quo. The unfinished fight for LGBTQ rights is a testament to his enduring influence and the relentless pursuit of a world where love knows no bounds.

Index

ability, 7, 26, 33, 42, 52, 54
absurdity, 26, 31
acceptance, 3–6, 8, 10, 14–16, 23, 25, 26, 29–31, 33–35, 48, 53, 58, 61, 66, 70, 71
act, 3, 5, 7, 13, 14, 18, 26, 42, 43, 52, 71
action, 41, 70
activism, 1, 2, 4, 6–8, 10, 13, 14, 16, 18, 20, 25, 29–31, 33, 35, 37, 40, 41, 49, 51–54, 58–66, 68, 69
activist, 2, 8, 14, 50, 63
actor, 22
addition, 42, 44, 60, 64, 65, 68
address, 20, 33, 35
adolescence, 2
adversity, 8
advocacy, 7, 26, 53, 68
advocate, 4, 12, 16, 26, 35, 46, 48, 66
aesthetic, 45
affront, 20, 28, 52
age, 4, 13
aggression, 4, 30
Alejandro Zambra, 46, 48
alliance, 14
anniversary, 66
Apocalipsis, 26

approach, 10, 18, 25, 29, 30, 42, 61, 63, 64, 69
approval, 20
archival, 68
archiving, 66
area, 23
arrival, 19
art, 1, 3–5, 7–11, 14, 17, 18, 23, 25, 26, 28–33, 42, 43, 45, 46, 49, 51–53, 58, 59, 61, 63–68, 70, 71
artist, 10, 14, 17, 50
artistry, 1
aspect, 42
assertion, 13, 54
atmosphere, 2, 6, 65
attempt, 52
attention, 7, 9, 68
attire, 7
attraction, 13
audience, 25, 26, 43
Augusto Pinochet, 2, 6, 20, 38
authenticity, 5, 43
autobiography, 41
awakening, 6
awareness, 13, 33, 70

backdrop, 1, 2, 13, 22, 37, 54

background, 2–5
backlash, 10, 20, 33, 42, 47, 51, 54, 58
barrier, 31
battle, 6
battleground, 4, 16
beacon, 6, 49, 66
beauty, 5, 18
beginning, 2, 8, 24
behavior, 4
being, 6, 29
bell, 46
binary, 5
blend, 8, 26, 37, 41, 46
blending, 38
body, 66
boldness, 29, 46
bond, 14
boy, 1
bravery, 52
bullying, 3
Butler, 25, 45

call, 9, 34, 41
camp, 9
campaign, 20
canon, 44–46, 63
career, 47, 53
catalyst, 1, 14, 28, 51
cause, 70
caution, 14
celebration, 6, 9, 13
censorship, 28, 42, 48, 51–54, 58, 67
center, 52
century, 19, 20
challenge, 3, 7, 9, 10, 13, 17, 28, 29, 33, 44, 46, 48, 54, 63, 64, 66, 68, 71

change, 2, 4, 10, 12, 14, 18, 26–28, 48, 50, 51, 63
childhood, 2, 3, 5, 13
Chile, 1, 2, 4, 6–10, 13, 14, 16, 18–26, 28–31, 35, 37–39, 41, 42, 46, 48–54, 57, 58, 61, 63–68
choice, 5
chronicle, 66
citizen, 2
city, 1, 2
clarion, 34
clash, 51
class, 1–5, 7, 8, 10, 13
climate, 2, 8, 9, 20
coexist, 45
collaboration, 4, 70
collective, 4, 6, 8–10, 14, 29, 32, 64, 66, 70
colonization, 22
color, 69
combination, 19, 30
coming, 13–16
commentary, 29, 38, 43
commitment, 6, 10, 14, 25, 26, 64, 68, 70
community, 3–10, 13, 14, 16–21, 23, 25, 26, 28, 30–35, 39–42, 50, 52, 61, 64–66, 68–70
complexity, 6, 18
complicity, 26, 31, 43
concept, 4, 25, 30
conclusion, 4, 10, 14, 21, 23, 26, 30, 31, 33, 35, 39, 41, 42, 46, 49, 50, 61, 63, 64, 66
confine, 26
conflict, 32
conformity, 32

Index 75

connection, 17
consumption, 52
contemporary, 21, 29, 42, 48, 61, 64
content, 10, 50, 53
context, 3, 10, 14, 19, 21, 22, 25, 30, 31, 38, 41, 42, 54, 61, 64, 67
continuation, 20
contrast, 2
control, 30, 54
conversation, 42
cornerstone, 64
counter, 31, 47
country, 17, 21, 23, 28, 39
coup, 2
courage, 6
craft, 38, 39
creation, 68
creativity, 42, 61, 70
criticism, 63
critique, 23, 25, 26, 29–31, 38, 42, 43, 45, 47, 59, 60
crucible, 13
cry, 26
culture, 3–6, 9, 12, 17, 21, 25, 26, 30, 31, 53, 60, 70
curricula, 60, 70

danger, 17
death, 66
decision, 3
declaration, 29
decriminalization, 24
defiance, 3, 5, 6, 9, 13, 18, 25, 43, 49, 53, 54, 61, 64, 71
definition, 30
democracy, 20
departure, 59
depth, 26

desire, 3, 5–7, 13, 14
determination, 42, 58
dialogue, 7, 10, 18, 23, 33, 41, 43, 57
dichotomy, 13, 52
dictatorship, 2, 9, 20, 24, 31, 38
dignity, 4, 21
disapproval, 13
discomfort, 51
disconnection, 16
discourse, 14, 22, 28–30, 45, 46, 48, 49, 52, 54, 57–59, 61–63, 66
discovery, 5, 6, 13
discrimination, 3, 6, 7, 9, 10, 12, 14, 19–24, 26, 29, 33, 54, 57, 64, 69
disdain, 30
dissent, 2, 6
diversity, 33
doctrine, 22
dominance, 5
drag, 9
dress, 43
duality, 3, 13, 17

ecstasy, 13
education, 22
effort, 54
elitism, 8
embrace, 3, 5, 8, 10, 26, 29, 48, 68
emergence, 24, 29, 35, 37, 38, 46
emotion, 7, 18
empathy, 58
employment, 21
empowerment, 10, 28, 29
end, 20
endeavor, 4, 13, 35
enforcement, 8
engagement, 40–42, 66

entrance, 6
entry, 8
environment, 1, 5, 8, 12, 16, 17, 20, 23, 26, 54
equality, 4, 10, 11, 21, 23–26, 29, 30, 32, 33, 35, 49, 53, 58, 61, 64, 66, 71
equation, 21, 47
era, 2, 20, 21, 24
erasure, 67
escape, 31
essence, 3, 25
establishment, 38, 51
estrangement, 15
Eve Kosofsky Sedgwick, 45
event, 20
evolution, 39
exaggeration, 9, 31
examination, 12, 23, 33
example, 5, 26, 29, 32, 33, 43, 69
exclusion, 33
exhibition, 52
existence, 5, 28, 29, 39
expectation, 14
experience, 13, 16, 33, 42, 46, 69
exploration, 5, 13, 14, 17, 31, 39, 48, 59
expression, 2, 25, 28–30, 33, 34, 40, 42, 43, 45, 51, 53, 54, 57, 58

fabric, 22, 28, 41
face, 5, 8, 21, 33, 53, 54
family, 1, 5, 16, 17, 21, 22
fear, 2, 5, 13, 14, 16, 20, 48
fellow, 9, 14, 17, 51
femininity, 9
fiction, 41

fight, 2, 4–8, 11, 14, 21, 23–26, 29–31, 33, 35, 41, 46, 48, 49, 53, 54, 58, 61, 65, 66, 68, 70, 71
figure, 39, 42, 48, 54, 60, 62
firm, 58
flair, 42
flamboyance, 9
flourishing, 38
fluidity, 63
force, 8, 18, 46
forefront, 30
form, 6, 17, 29, 30, 38, 45, 53, 64
formation, 47
Foucault, 54
foundation, 64
founding, 4, 10, 64
framework, 3, 22, 30, 39, 54
Francisco Casas, 14
freedom, 48, 50–54, 58
function, 47
future, 4, 10, 11, 18, 31, 43, 52, 53, 61, 63, 64, 66, 68, 70

gain, 68
gay, 6, 38
gender, 4, 5, 8–10, 12, 25, 31–33, 42, 43, 45, 47, 63, 64
generation, 29, 35, 46, 48, 49, 58
geography, 61
glimpse, 5, 14
globe, 39, 61, 68
Gloria Anzaldúa, 46
government, 2, 20
gratitude, 65
groundwork, 35, 46
group, 9, 29, 64

harassment, 8

Index   77

hardship, 3
harm, 31
hate, 20
hatred, 32
head, 29
heart, 4, 25
heartbreak, 14
heteronormativity, 9, 13, 15
heterosexuality, 5, 30
hierarchy, 32
history, 10, 19, 21, 31, 70
Homi K. Bhabha, 47
homophobia, 9, 26, 29, 31–34, 60, 64
homosexuality, 3, 7, 14, 24, 32
honesty, 18
honor, 61, 64, 66
hope, 2, 5, 6, 20, 49, 66
hostility, 1, 8, 42, 51
humor, 6, 7, 9, 26, 31
hypocrisy, 23

idea, 13, 14, 18, 25
identity, 1–6, 8–10, 13, 14, 16–18, 22, 25, 26, 28, 29, 32, 33, 39–42, 46–49, 54, 57, 59, 63, 68
imagery, 42
impact, 2, 26, 28, 30, 40, 41, 46–49, 59, 61, 63, 65
importance, 6, 13, 30, 33, 40, 41, 46, 53, 54, 61, 63, 65, 66
imprisonment, 20
incident, 52
inclusion, 46
inclusivity, 8, 10, 31, 33–35, 43, 61, 64
incorporation, 42
individual, 2, 3, 14, 23, 51

individuality, 43
inequality, 1, 29, 69
influence, 2, 4, 5, 21–23, 29, 39, 41, 48, 60, 63, 68, 71
injustice, 58
innovation, 42
insight, 64, 68
insistence, 35
inspiration, 6, 9, 18, 29, 41, 42, 68
instance, 3, 7, 21, 22, 28, 66
institution, 22
intent, 51
interconnectedness, 40
interest, 59, 60
internalization, 32
interplay, 14, 21, 23, 25, 39, 42
intersection, 16
intersectionality, 3, 4, 6, 21, 35, 46, 69
intertextuality, 42
intimacy, 13
introspection, 33
involvement, 4, 7
ire, 10, 53
issue, 21, 22

Jean Genet, 42
journey, 2, 4–6, 8, 13, 14, 16, 23–25, 39, 41, 50, 66
joy, 16
Judith Butler, 25, 47, 63
Judith Butler, 45
justice, 4, 7, 10, 11, 14, 25, 52, 61, 64, 66, 69, 71

knowledge, 54, 64

lack, 54

landscape, 1–3, 6, 8, 10, 16, 23, 25, 26, 34, 38, 39, 46, 47, 49, 50, 54, 64
law, 8, 20, 24
legacy, 8, 10, 25, 26, 29–31, 33, 35, 41, 43, 46–49, 53, 54, 58, 59, 61, 63–66, 68, 70
legalization, 21, 22
legislation, 70
Lemebel, 1–8, 10, 12–14, 17, 18, 23, 25, 26, 28–35, 38–43, 45–54, 57–68, 70, 71
lens, 2, 5, 7, 30, 45, 47, 54, 64
liberation, 14, 15
life, 1–7, 13, 14, 17, 18, 35, 59, 64–66, 68, 70
lifetime, 48, 54, 61
light, 54
like, 6, 7, 23, 25, 37, 46, 63, 64
Lina Meruane, 46, 48
literature, 8, 23, 28, 29, 37–42, 44, 46, 48–50, 54, 59–66
loss, 14, 48
love, 6, 8, 13, 14, 16–18, 29, 48, 66, 71
luminary, 25

machismo, 4, 6, 9, 13, 15, 17, 25, 26, 29, 31, 34, 43, 60, 64
mainstream, 9
makeup, 43
man, 5, 6, 16, 38, 41
manhood, 30
marginalization, 5, 23
mark, 8, 10, 26
marriage, 21, 22, 24
masculinity, 1, 4, 9, 26, 30–32, 63
meaning, 59
means, 3, 33, 41

media, 52
medium, 43
memory, 61, 66, 68, 71
message, 28, 43, 58
Michel Foucault, 64
Michel Foucault's, 54
milestone, 20
mirror, 5, 14, 50
mission, 9, 35
moment, 5, 10, 15
moral, 19, 23, 28
morality, 28
movement, 4, 6–8, 10, 33, 40, 42, 48, 51, 57, 64, 70
multiplicity, 46
mural, 65

name, 9
narrative, 6, 26, 29, 31, 38, 39, 41, 42, 46, 47, 52, 54, 58, 68
nation, 1, 2, 39
nature, 15, 21, 31, 33, 63
necessity, 53, 54
need, 8, 21, 28
negotiation, 17
neighborhood, 3, 13, 65
network, 41
norm, 6
notion, 25, 45, 66

observer, 7
Ocean Vuong, 40
oeuvre, 44
on, 1–4, 8, 10, 22, 25, 26, 29–31, 33, 35, 40, 43, 46, 48, 49, 51, 54, 58, 60–63, 65, 66, 68, 70, 71
one, 6, 28, 33, 42, 51, 52, 54, 64
opinion, 52, 57, 58

opposition, 20, 21, 24
oppression, 1–3, 40, 48, 53, 65
order, 44
orientation, 10, 33
ostracism, 21
ostracization, 13
other, 17, 33, 51, 69
output, 17
outrage, 52

parade, 20
part, 6, 33, 35, 42, 52, 64, 68
participation, 29
partnership, 14, 17
passage, 20
passing, 59, 61, 64–66
passion, 2, 17, 18
past, 10, 68
path, 14, 16, 18
Pedro, 16
Pedro Lemebel, 1, 8, 10, 14, 23, 25, 37, 52, 54, 57, 59, 63, 65, 66, 68
Pedro Lemebel's, 2, 4, 6, 8, 13, 14, 16, 18, 25, 26, 28, 30, 31, 33–35, 39, 41, 42, 44, 46, 49, 50, 53, 58, 61, 63, 64, 70
Peggy Phelan, 25
perception, 52
performance, 4, 5, 7, 9, 10, 17, 23, 25–29, 31, 32, 42, 43, 45, 46, 49, 58
performativity, 25, 45
period, 6
persecution, 6, 14
persona, 6
personal, 2, 4–6, 13–15, 18, 22, 26, 29, 31, 38–40, 42

perspective, 5, 7, 29
phenomenon, 32
philosophy, 25
piece, 71
pilgrimage, 65
Pinochet, 9, 31
place, 9
platform, 4, 5, 9, 26, 33
poetry, 46, 59
policy, 22
position, 10, 28, 41, 42, 51, 62
possibility, 5, 14
potential, 10, 13, 15
poverty, 3
power, 4, 6, 10, 14, 27, 30, 42, 47–49, 51–54, 58, 59, 63–65, 70
precedent, 52
prejudice, 32, 33
preservation, 67
pressure, 52
prevalent, 29, 32
pride, 5, 13, 20, 29
process, 13
progress, 8, 25, 52, 63
promise, 2
prose, 46, 59
protest, 29
provocateur, 52, 63
prowess, 58
public, 8, 9, 13, 22–24, 28–30, 42, 48, 52, 57, 58, 65, 66
punk, 9
pursuit, 35, 43, 71

quality, 45
queer, 1–7, 9, 10, 13, 14, 16–18, 25, 28, 29, 32, 33, 39–42, 45–48, 52, 59–63, 70

queerness, 1, 29
quest, 2, 4, 21, 25
quo, 2, 3, 5, 7, 9, 13, 20, 23, 25, 29, 31, 46, 51, 54, 57, 63, 71

race, 8, 10
racism, 69
rallying, 26
range, 42
rawness, 3
reach, 60
reading, 42
reality, 13, 16
realm, 25
reassessment, 61
rebellion, 5, 13, 18
reception, 47, 48, 50
recognition, 4, 20, 21, 23, 24, 35, 46, 61
redefinition, 45
reevaluation, 31, 46
reference, 61
reflection, 41, 43, 53
regime, 2, 6, 9, 20, 31
regulation, 54
rejection, 5, 9, 13, 16, 32
relationship, 14, 17, 64
relevance, 59, 62
religion, 22
reminder, 6, 10, 33, 48, 53, 59, 61, 63, 65
removal, 52
representation, 28, 46–49, 54, 60, 61, 63, 64
repression, 2, 30, 31, 38, 42
reservoir, 39
reshaping, 28, 29
resilience, 6, 8, 21, 23, 25, 30, 54, 58, 64

resistance, 3, 4, 9, 10, 13, 17, 22–26, 29, 30, 38, 39, 41, 42, 46, 48, 51–53, 64
resolve, 2, 14
response, 6, 9, 51, 70
resurgence, 59
rethinking, 44
retribution, 48
revelation, 15
revival, 60
rhetoric, 21, 52
right, 42, 52, 54, 58
rise, 2
risk, 67
rock, 9
role, 5, 21, 22, 29, 41, 50–52, 57, 63
rule, 31

Salvador Allende's, 2
sanctity, 22
Santiago, 1–5, 7, 13, 14, 16, 20, 65
Sarah Schulman, 40
satire, 6, 7, 26, 29, 31, 43, 45
scale, 60
scene, 9
secrecy, 13
section, 19, 46, 51, 59, 61, 66
self, 3, 4, 6, 15, 17, 29, 32
sense, 3, 4, 9, 10, 13, 16, 23, 29, 33, 40, 64
sentiment, 10
series, 23, 25, 45, 53
serve, 25, 31, 38, 46, 48, 50, 59, 61, 63, 64, 68
set, 2, 19, 52
sex, 19–22
sexism, 69

Index 81

sexuality, 1, 3–5, 9, 12–14, 17, 22, 25, 26, 31, 39, 42, 45, 47, 48, 57, 59, 63, 64
shame, 3
shaming, 31
shape, 7, 20
shift, 2, 10, 30, 46, 48
shock, 5, 7, 43
side, 51
significance, 46, 61, 63
silence, 3, 5, 7, 9, 18, 30, 42, 51, 53, 54, 67
site, 25, 42, 65
society, 1–7, 9, 10, 13, 16–18, 21, 23, 25, 26, 28–32, 34, 35, 41, 47, 51, 54, 57, 60, 61, 64
socio, 1, 2, 6, 9, 16, 21, 23, 39, 41, 67
solace, 6, 13
solidarity, 4, 8–10, 13, 16, 29, 33, 40, 41, 52, 64, 68, 70
source, 3, 16, 18, 41
space, 6, 9, 10, 17, 23, 29, 45, 63
spectrum, 13, 33
sphere, 46
spirit, 4, 10, 61, 66, 71
stage, 2
stake, 52
state, 2, 20, 22, 66
statement, 15, 54
status, 2, 3, 5, 7, 9, 13, 20, 23, 25, 29, 31, 46, 48, 51, 54, 57, 63, 71
step, 20, 24, 68
stigma, 14, 29, 32
story, 14, 16, 52
street, 3, 9
strength, 3, 5, 33
structure, 21

struggle, 2, 4, 6, 8, 9, 13, 14, 20, 23, 25, 30, 32, 33, 35, 52, 54, 58, 61, 63, 65, 66, 68
study, 60
style, 6, 29, 33, 39, 41, 42, 48, 65
success, 10
summary, 2, 18, 58
support, 17
sway, 9

taboo, 7, 12, 28, 46, 64
tapestry, 2, 8, 13, 39, 41, 66
task, 20, 68
technique, 31
technology, 70
teenager, 2
tension, 17, 20, 33, 50, 51
terror, 20
testament, 4, 6, 18, 23, 25, 30, 63, 71
theatricality, 6
theme, 32
theory, 42, 45, 47, 54, 59, 63, 70
thought, 61
thread, 41
thrill, 13
time, 3, 4, 6, 13, 38, 61
today, 10, 70
tool, 4, 7, 10, 27, 30, 31, 41
torch, 68
torture, 20
touchstone, 60
tradition, 37–39
trait, 4
transformation, 28
transgender, 32, 69
transition, 20
truth, 6, 33

understanding, 4–6, 13, 14, 16–18, 26, 31, 37, 46
union, 20
unity, 8
universality, 48
university, 62
upbringing, 1, 2
upheaval, 2
urgency, 9, 13
use, 9, 26, 31, 43

validity, 47
value, 5, 7, 43, 46
variety, 9
vehicle, 4, 14
vibrancy, 37
vigilance, 25
violence, 2, 6, 8, 9, 14, 17, 23, 31, 69
Virginia Woolf, 42
visibility, 5, 13, 20, 28, 30, 48, 61, 63
voice, 2, 3, 28, 39, 41, 42, 53, 54, 57, 64, 68, 71
vulnerability, 26, 31

warrior, 10, 64
wave, 2
way, 4, 10, 17, 40, 46, 48, 60, 63
weapon, 5, 25
well, 66
whole, 31
willingness, 16
window, 14
work, 2, 4, 5, 7, 11, 12, 14, 18, 25, 26, 28–31, 33–35, 38, 39, 41, 42, 45–49, 51, 54, 59–61, 63, 64, 66–68, 70
working, 1–5, 7, 13
world, 3, 8, 11, 14, 18, 30, 41, 46, 59, 71
worldview, 2, 3
writer, 2, 3, 50, 63, 64
writing, 3, 4, 16, 31, 41, 42, 49

Yeguas, 7
Yeguas del Apocalipsis, 9, 10
youth, 2